Name of Business _____

For Tax Year _____

Small Business Made Sir

Small Business Bookkeeping System Simplified

by **Daniel Sitarz**
Attorney-at-Law

Nova Publishing Company

Small Business and Consumer Legal Books and Software
Carbondale, Illinois

Editorial assistance by Janet Harris Sitarz, Linda Jorgensen-Buhman, and Melanie Bray. Interior design by Linda Jorgensen-Buhman. Manufactured in the United States.

ISBN 0-935755-74-8   Book only   ($14.95)

Cataloging-in-Publication Data
    Sitarz, Dan, 1948-
        Small Business Bookkeeping System Simplified / by Daniel Sitarz. -- 1st ed.
        128 p. cm. -- (Small Business Made Simple series).
        1. Bookkeeping—United States—Popular Works. 2. Bookkeeping—United States—
        Forms. 3. Bookkeeping—United States—States—Popular Works. I. Sitarz, Daniel.
        II. Title. III. Series.
        ISBN 0-935755-74-8, Book only ($14.95).

Nova Publishing Company is dedicated to providing up-to-date and accurate legal information to the public. All Nova publications are periodically revised to contain the latest available legal information.

1st Edition; 1st Printing   September, 2003

This publication is designed to provide accurate and authoritative information in regard to the subject matter covered. It is sold with the understanding that the publisher and author are not engaged in rendering legal, accounting, or other professional services. If legal advice or other expert assistance is required, the services of a competent professional person should be sought.

> —From a Declaration of Principles jointly adopted by a Committee of
> the American Bar Association and a Committee of Publishers

DISCLAIMER

Because of possible unanticipated changes in governing statutes and case law relating to the application of any information contained in this book, the author, publisher, and any and all persons or entities involved in any way in the preparation, publication, sale, or distribution of this book disclaim all responsibility for the legal effects or consequences of any document prepared or action taken in reliance upon information contained in this book. No representations, either express or implied, are made or given regarding the legal consequences of the use of any information contained in this book. Purchasers and persons intending to use this book for the preparation of any legal documents are advised to check specifically on the current applicable laws in any jurisdiction in which they intend the documents to be effective.

Nova Publishing Company
Small Business and Consumer Legal Books and Software
1103 West College Street
Carbondale, IL 62901
Editorial: (800) 748-1175

Distributed by:
National Book Network
4501 Forbes Blvd.
Lanham, MD 20706
Orders: (800) 462-6420

Table of Contents

Instructions for Using Bookkeeping Records

The bookkeeping system used in this book is a calendar year-based modified single-entry accounting system. It is designed as a cash-basis accounting system that can be used by any business with less than $1 million annual income. The IRS has determined that this type of accounting system is "relatively simple ... and adequate for income tax purposes." This system has been designed to make accuracy, clarity, and ease-of-use its primary objectives. Upon completion of the year (December 31), you will have the information necessary for the following reports:

- **Balance Sheet**: This basic form is used to keep track of what a business owes (its *debts* or *liabilities*) and what a business owns (its *property* or *assets*). If money is owed to the business, these are called *accounts receivable*. If the business owes money to others, these are called *accounts payable*. What the value of the business is to the owner is called the *equity* of a business. Equity is considered a liability or debt of the business, even though it is only owed to the owner of the business. The basic equation for business accounting is: *Assets – Liabilities = Equity*. On a balance sheet, both sides of this equation must be equal. You will complete this form at the end of your calendar year.
- **Profit and Loss Statement:** This is the other main business report, sometimes called an *income* or *operating statement*. It is used to keep track of any money received (*income*) or money paid out (*expenses*) for your business. For any period of time: *Income – Expenses = Profit*. You will complete this form at the end of your calendar year.

Setting Up Additional Expense Accounts

Following these instructions, you will see a completed sample Weekly Expense and Income Record. In the right-hand column on the right-hand sample page, please note that under "Expense Totals," an additional sample expense account (#26: Tuition) was set up to allow the business owner to specifically keep track of expenses for tuition for a business course at a local community college. There are two unused expense accounts on the income & expense record that you may use to keep track of any specific expenses for your business that do not fit in any of the other account classifications: Accounts #26 and #27.

Weekly Expense and Income Record Instructions

To complete each week takes five simple steps:

① **Enter Expense Transactions:** You will need to enter every transaction when you spend money for your business. These transactions are your *Expenses*. For each expense, you will enter an account number that corresponds to the correct account under which the expense will be totaled. For example, if you spend $50.00 for repairs during a week, you would enter this expense under the *General Expenses* column on the left-hand page for that week. You would enter the date of the payment, the name of whom you paid and description of what you paid for (if necessary, to make clear what the expense was), the check number or credit card used for payment, the account number for "Repairs/Maintenance" (Account #20 from the *Expense Totals* box in the right-hand column on the right-hand page), and finally, the amount paid. Specific instructions about each type of expense account are outlined on the next pages. (*Note*: If the expenses are for *Inventory*, *Equipment/Property*, or *Payroll*, they will be entered in the appropriate box on the left-hand page. All other expenses are entered under the *General Expenses* area on the left-hand page.

② **Enter Income Transactions:** You will also need to enter every transaction when you receive money in your business. This is your *Income*. These transactions are entered on the left-hand column of the right-hand page under "Weekly Income or Returns." You should enter the date you received the income, the name of who paid (or just enter "Daily Revenue" for a business with lots of cash transactions each day), the check number of a payment or a notation that the payment was cash, and the appropriate *Income Account* number from the *Income Totals* box below the *Weekly Income or Returns* area. The types of Income Accounts are as follows:

- **Sales of Goods Income**: From the sale of inventory (material, merchandise, parts, or goods)
- **Service/Labor Income**: From any labor or services you provide (*Note*: An individual amount of income may have separate portions that are attributable to sales income and service income. These amounts need to be recorded separately

③ **Enter Payroll Transactions:** If you have any employees, you will need to complete a Employee Payroll Record for each employee. These follow the Weekly Expense and Income Records. To complete this form, see the instructions later under "Employee Payroll Record." From your completed Employee Payroll Records, you will enter information onto your Weekly Expense and Income Record under *Payroll Expenses* on the left-hand page.

④ **Enter Expense and Income Totals:** After you have entered all of your expenses, income, and payroll information for the week, you will need to total the amounts for each account category and enter the total in the appropriate area under "Expense Totals" or "Income Totals" on the right-hand page. For example, if you have made three purchases of supplies during the week (Expense Account #23), you would add the three amounts together to come up with a total for the Supplies/Tools category. You would then write that amount in the "Total for Week" column to the right of Expense Account #23: Supplies/Tools. Continue to do this for all of your expense and income transactions for the week.

⑤ **Calculate Totals to Date and Carry Totals to the Next Week**: For your first week in business, you will have no *Prior Week Total* amount. For that week, simply re-enter your *Total for Week* amounts in the *Total to Date* column and add all of the category entries for the *Total for Week* space at the bottom of the column. Next, re-enter the figures from the *Total to Date* column on the next week's *Prior Week Total* column (on the next page) for each expense and income category. For all of the following weeks, you will need to add the amounts in the *Prior Week Total* to the amounts in the *Total for Week* column for each category and enter the sum in the *Total to Date* Column. Again, when completed, recopy the *Total to Date* figures to the next week's *Prior Week Total* column (on the next page).

Checking Your Calculations

① Total the *Expense Total for Week* amounts from your weekly *General Expenses*, *Inventory Expenses*, *Equipment/Property Expenses*, and *Payroll* boxes on the left-hand page. This amount should equal the *Total for Week* amount at the bottom of your *Expense Totals*. If there are discrepancies, check your calculations when you totaled the amounts for each category and also check to see that you have transferred the amounts correctly to the *Expense Totals* columns for each category

② Your *Total for Week* amount in the *Weekly Income or Returns* section should equal the *Total for Week* amount at the bottom of your *Income Totals* area. If there are discrepancies, check your calculations when you totaled the amounts for each category and also check to see that you have transferred the amounts correctly to the *Income Totals* columns for each category.

Expense Account Instructions

Non-deductible Expenses

Expenses under these listings are not directly deductible as business expenses.

① **Inventory**: All of the purchases or costs of any materials or merchandise that you have for sale. These expenses are not deductible as such, but are deductible as the "cost of goods sold," explained later.

② **Equipment/Property:** Purchases of equipment and/or real estate to be used in a business (including cars, trucks, furniture, computers, etc.). These items are also not deductible as such, but are generally deductible as special IRS Section 179 expenses, currently up to a total of $25,000.00. Check with an up-to-date tax manual or a competent tax advisor for details.

③ **Loans/Notes Paid:** Amounts spent to pay off the principal of any loans or notes are not deductible. Any amounts spent on interest on such loans or notes, however, are deductible under Account #13: Interest Paid.

④ **Federal Income Tax**: Amounts paid by a business for federal income tax are not deductible.

⑤ **Personal Expense**: Any money spent on non-business personal expenses of the owners is not deductible.

⑥ This account is left blank and may be used for any other non-deductible expense items, such as a salary that a sole proprietor or partner takes from the business.

Deductible Expenses

Expenses under the following listings are deductible as business expenses.

⑦ **Advertising**: Expenses for advertising, promotions, and marketing for your business.

⑧ **Auto/Truck/Travel**: Expenses related to using a vehicle for business purposes and for any other travel expenses. At printing of this book, businesses are allowed a $.36 per mile deduction for business-related travel. Check with the IRS for current mileage rates.

⑨ **Bank Fees**: Expenses related to checking, checks, or savings accounts, including service charges.

⑩ **Contributions**: Expenses for any charitable contributions. (The deductibility of these are limited for sole proprietorships and partnerships).

⑪ **Lodging**: Expenses related to spending the night away from home for business-related purposes.

⑫ **Insurance**: Expenses related to insurance coverage for the business. If you are using a home office, expenses are deductible in relation to the percentage of square footage of the home office compared to the entire home.

⑬ **Interest Paid**: Expenses for any interest paid out for business loans, business-related credit card charges, etc.

⑭ **Legal/Professional**: Any legal, accounting, or other professional service expenses the business may need.

⑮ **Meals/Entertainment**: Expenses for meals and entertainment of clients. Only 50 percent of these expenses are deductible.

⑯ **Payroll (Net Pay)**: The amount for this listing should be the net pay for all employees, after the deductions for Social Security, Medicare, and federal, state and/or local withholding taxes are taken.

⑰ **Payroll (Deductions)**: The amount for this listing should be the monthly payment deposit amount, as shown on the Payroll Tax Depository Record, and any checks written for state or local withholding taxes. (*Note*: Enter as expenses only when you have actually paid the monthly federal tax deposit or any state or local payroll taxes.

⑱ **Postage/Freight**: Any postage, express delivery services, shipping costs, or other freight charges expenses.

⑲ **Rent**: Expenses paid for rent of an office, office furniture, tools, or any other periodic rental.

⑳ **Repairs/Maintenance**: Expenses for repair or maintenance of any business-related equipment or property.

㉑ **Taxes (Sales)**: The amount of any state sales tax collected. Check with your state revenue department.

㉒ **Taxes (Other)**: The amount of any other taxes paid by the business (other than federal income tax—see account #4 above). The home office share of any real estate taxes for a home is deductible.

㉓ **Supplies/Tools**: Expenses for the purchase of any business supplies and/or tools used in the business.

㉔ **Telephone/Internet**: Expenses for any phone, fax, or internet connection and monthly charges.

㉕ **Utilities**: The business share of any other utilities, such as water, sewer, trash, electric, gas, etc.

㉖ & ㉗ These accounts are left blank and may be used for any other deductible expense items. Any expenses that are necessary for your business to operate and are normal for your type of business are generally deductible. You may wish to name one of these accounts "Miscellaneous."

Instructions for Other Recordkeeping Sheets

Payroll Instructions

- **Employee Payroll Record**: There are records for up to four employees, with one employee per page. If more records are needed, you may wish to use Nova's *Small Business Payroll System Simplified* for up to 20 employees. Fill in the name, address, Social Security number, rate of pay, and number of exemptions for each employee. Each week, enter the hours worked and multiply by the pay rate for the gross pay. To determine the deductions for federal income tax, Social Security and Medicare, you will need an up-to-date copy of IRS Circular E (Publication 15): *Employer's Tax Guide.*

- **Monthly Payroll Summary**: Carry the totals for all employees from each individual Employee Payroll Record to the correct columns for each month on this annual form. This information is necessary to complete IRS Form 941: *Employer's Quarterly Federal Tax Return.*

- **Payroll Tax Depository Record**: This form is used to determine the amount for each monthly required payroll tax deposit. These deposits are made at your local bank using IRS Form 8109: *Federal Tax Deposit Coupon* and are required if your monthly payroll is over $500.00. On this form each month, enter the total federal tax, Social Security, and Medicare taxes withheld for all employees (taken from the Monthly Payroll Summary) that are the employee shares. The amounts to enter for the "Employer Share" columns for Social Security and Medicare are the same amounts listed in the "Employee Share" columns. Total the columns across and pay this amount as a deposit each month.

- **Annual Inventory Record**: Complete this form in January of each year for all of the current material or goods that you had in stock as of December 31. The Annual Inventory Record requires a physical count of the inventory items on hand at the end of the calendar year. The total from this form is used in the Cost of Goods Sold calculation below.

- **Annual Cost of Goods Sold Record**: Also complete this form in January each year. Insert the inventory value from the beginning of the year (zero in your first year of business and the prior year end-of-year total for all later years). Add the total inventory added during the year (Final Expense Account #1 amount). From this total, subtract the inventory value at the end of the year (from your Annual Inventory Record) to arrive at your Cost of Goods Sold amount for the year.

- **Annual Accounts Payable Summary**: Complete this in January also. Enter amounts for any vendors that you owe money to at the end of the year. (This sheet may be needed by your tax preparer, if necessary, to convert your records from a Cash method of bookkeeping to an Accrual method).

- **Annual Accounts Receivable Summary**: Complete this in January also. Enter amounts for any customers that owe you money at the end of the year. (This sheet may be needed by your tax preparer, if needed, to convert your records from a Cash method of bookkeeping to an Accrual method).

- **Annual Property and Equipment Summary:** Use this sheet to track any equipment bought or sold during the year and any property or equipment casualty losses (from damage or theft). For "depreciation" amounts, you will need to consult a tax advisor. The *cost basis* of a piece of property or equipment is normally the original cost of the item minus any depreciation deduction that has been claimed for the property. *Selling expenses* are any fees, commissions, etc. that were needed to sell the property or equipment.

- **Annual Profit and Loss Statement**: Fill in the appropriate dollar amounts from your final week of the year Expense Totals and Income Totals taken from your Weekly Expense and Income Record sheets. The Cost of Goods Sold amount will come from your Annual Cost of Goods Sold Record. Follow the calculation explanations where necessary.

- **Annual Balance Sheet**: Complete this in January of each year. Take the appropriate dollar amounts from the correct entries on the previous annual summary sheets and/or from loan or credit card statements. Follow the calculation explanations where necessary.

- **Annual Summary for Tax Preparation**: This sheet is designed to provide your tax preparer with most of the information necessary to complete your taxes each year. You may also need to provide some of the other Annual Summary sheets if necessary. Enter the amounts from your final week of the year Expense Totals and Income Totals from your Weekly Expense and Income Record sheets and from any appropriate Annual Summary sheets.

- **Tax Forms Checklist**: Check through this list to determine which tax forms are necessary for the type of entity of your business (sole proprietorship, partnership, limited liability company, S-corporation, or standard C-corporation). IRS Publication 334: *Tax Guide for Small Business* is also very useful. You may order any of the tax forms via 1-(800)-TAXFORM or www.irs.gov/formspubs

WEEKLY EXPENSE AND INCOME RECORD

Week Ending On _June 19_ , 20 _04_

GENERAL EXPENSES

Date	Name and Description	Check # or Credit Card	Acct #	Amount	
14	Office Max	1116	23	267	15
15	Verizon	1117	24	94	20
16	Able Supply	1119	23	116	37
17	Carson Rentals	1121	19	400	00
18	USPS	1122	18	127	50
18	Target Radio	1123	7	600	00
19	Baker College	Visa	26	100	00
	Total for Week			1705	22

INVENTORY EXPENSES

Date	Name and Description	Check # or Credit Card	Acct #	Amount	
17	Carl's Electronics	1118	1	750	00
18	Packaging.com	Visa	1	1000	00
			1		
			1		
			1		
			1		
			1		
			1		
			1		
			1		
			1		
			1		
	Total for Week			1750	00

EQUIPMENT/PROPERTY EXPENSES

Date	Name and Description	Check # or Credit Card	Acct #	Amount	
17	Computer Max	1120	2	795	63
			2		
			2		
			2		
			2		
			2		
			2		
			2		
			2		
			2		
			2		
	Total for Week			795	63

PAYROLL EXPENSES

Date	Employee	Check #	Acct #	Net Pay	
14	Sharon Smith	1114	16	250	72
14	Bill Jones	1115	16	153	02
			16		
			16		
	Total for Week			403	74

WEEKLY EXPENSE AND INCOME RECORD

Week Ending On _____ , 20 _____

WEEKLY INCOME OR RETURNS

Date	Name and Description	Check # or Cash	Acct #	Amount	
Total for Week					

EXPENSE TOTALS

#	Account	Prior Week Total	Total for Week	Total to Date	
Non-Deductible Expenses					
1	Inventory				
2	Equipment/Property				
3	Loans/Notes Paid				
4	Federal Income Tax				
5	Personal Expense				
6					
	Sub-Total				

#	Account	Prior Week Total	Total for Week	Total to Date	
Deductible Expenses					
7	Advertising				
8	Auto/Truck/Travel				
9	Bank Fees				
10	Contributions				
11	Lodging				
12	Insurance				
13	Interest Paid				
14	Legal/Professional				
15	Meals/Entertainment				
16	Payroll (Net Pay)				
17	Payroll (Deductions)				
18	Postage/Freight				
19	Rent				
20	Repairs/Maintenance				
21	Taxes (Sales)				
22	Taxes (Other)				
23	Supplies/Tools				
24	Telephone/Internet				
25	Utilities				
26					
27					
	Sub-Total				

INCOME TOTALS

#	Account	Prior Week Total	Total for Week	Total to Date
1	Sale of Goods Income			
2	Service/Labor Income			
3	Miscellaneous Income			
4	Returns (deduct)	( )	( )	( )

Prior Week Total		
Total for Week		
Total to Date		

Prior Week Total		
Total for Week		
Total to Date		

WEEKLY EXPENSE AND INCOME RECORD

Week Ending On _____ , 20 ____

GENERAL EXPENSES

Date	Name and Description	Check # or Credit Card	Acct #	Amount	
	Total for Week				

INVENTORY EXPENSES

Date	Name and Description	Check # or Credit Card	Acct #	Amount	
			1		
			1		
			1		
			1		
			1		
			1		
			1		
			1		
			1		
			1		
			1		
			1		
	Total for Week				

EQUIPMENT/PROPERTY EXPENSES

Date	Name and Description	Check # or Credit Card	Acct #	Amount	
			2		
			2		
			2		
			2		
			2		
			2		
			2		
			2		
			2		
			2		
			2		
	Total for Week				

PAYROLL EXPENSES

Date	Employee	Check #	Acct #	Net Pay	
			16		
			16		
			16		
			16		
	Total for Week				

WEEKLY EXPENSE AND INCOME RECORD

Week Ending On _____ , 20 ____

WEEKLY INCOME OR RETURNS

Date	Name and Description	Check # or Cash	Acct #	Amount
	Total for Week			

INCOME TOTALS

#	Account	Prior Week Total	Total for Week	Total to Date
1	Sale of Goods Income			
2	Service/Labor Income			
3	Miscellaneous Income			
4	Returns (deduct)	( )	( )	( )

Prior Week Total	
Total for Week	
Total to Date	

EXPENSE TOTALS

#	Account	Prior Week Total	Total for Week	Total to Date
Non-Deductible Expenses				
1	Inventory			
2	Equipment/Property			
3	Loans/Notes Paid			
4	Federal Income Tax			
5	Personal Expense			
6				
	Sub-Total			

#	Account	Prior Week Total	Total for Week	Total to Date
Deductible Expenses				
7	Advertising			
8	Auto/Truck/Travel			
9	Bank Fees			
10	Contributions			
11	Lodging			
12	Insurance			
13	Interest Paid			
14	Legal/Professional			
15	Meals/Entertainment			
16	Payroll (Net Pay)			
17	Payroll (Deductions)			
18	Postage/Freight			
19	Rent			
20	Repairs/Maintenance			
21	Taxes (Sales)			
22	Taxes (Other)			
23	Supplies/Tools			
24	Telephone/Internet			
25	Utilities			
26				
27				
	Sub-Total			

Prior Week Total	
Total for Week	
Total to Date	

WEEKLY EXPENSE AND INCOME RECORD

Week Ending On _____ , 20 _____

GENERAL EXPENSES

Date	Name and Description	Check # or Credit Card	Acct #	Amount	
Total for Week					

INVENTORY EXPENSES

Date	Name and Description	Check # or Credit Card	Acct #	Amount	
			1		
			1		
			1		
			1		
			1		
			1		
			1		
			1		
			1		
			1		
			1		
			1		
Total for Week					

EQUIPMENT/PROPERTY EXPENSES

Date	Name and Description	Check # or Credit Card	Acct #	Amount	
			2		
			2		
			2		
			2		
			2		
			2		
			2		
			2		
			2		
			2		
			2		
Total for Week					

PAYROLL EXPENSES

Date	Employee	Check #	Acct #	Net Pay	
			16		
			16		
			16		
			16		
Total for Week					

WEEKLY EXPENSE AND INCOME RECORD

Week Ending On _____ , 20 _____

WEEKLY INCOME OR RETURNS

Date	Name and Description	Check # or Cash	Acct #	Amount
	Total for Week			

EXPENSE TOTALS

#	Account	Prior Week Total	Total for Week	Total to Date
Non-Deductible Expenses				
1	Inventory			
2	Equipment/Property			
3	Loans/Notes Paid			
4	Federal Income Tax			
5	Personal Expense			
6				
	Sub-Total			

#	Account	Prior Week Total	Total for Week	Total to Date
Deductible Expenses				
7	Advertising			
8	Auto/Truck/Travel			
9	Bank Fees			
10	Contributions			
11	Lodging			
12	Insurance			
13	Interest Paid			
14	Legal/Professional			
15	Meals/Entertainment			
16	Payroll (Net Pay)			
17	Payroll (Deductions)			
18	Postage/Freight			
19	Rent			
20	Repairs/Maintenance			
21	Taxes (Sales)			
22	Taxes (Other)			
23	Supplies/Tools			
24	Telephone/Internet			
25	Utilities			
26				
27				
	Sub-Total			

INCOME TOTALS

#	Account	Prior Week Total	Total for Week	Total to Date
1	Sale of Goods Income			
2	Service/Labor Income			
3	Miscellaneous Income			
4	Returns (deduct)	( )	( )	( )

Prior Week Total		
Total for Week		
Total to Date		

Prior Week Total		
Total for Week		
Total to Date		

WEEKLY EXPENSE AND INCOME RECORD

Week Ending On _____ , 20 _____

GENERAL EXPENSES

Date	Name and Description	Check # or Credit Card	Acct #	Amount
	Total for Week			

INVENTORY EXPENSES

Date	Name and Description	Check # or Credit Card	Acct #	Amount
			1	
			1	
			1	
			1	
			1	
			1	
			1	
			1	
			1	
			1	
			1	
			1	
		Total for Week		

EQUIPMENT/PROPERTY EXPENSES

Date	Name and Description	Check # or Credit Card	Acct #	Amount
			2	
			2	
			2	
			2	
			2	
			2	
			2	
			2	
			2	
			2	
			2	
		Total for Week		

PAYROLL EXPENSES

Date	Employee	Check #	Acct #	Net Pay
			16	
			16	
			16	
			16	
	Total for Week			

WEEKLY EXPENSE AND INCOME RECORD

Week Ending On _____ , 20 _____

WEEKLY INCOME OR RETURNS

Date	Name and Description	Check # or Cash	Acct #	Amount
Total for Week				

EXPENSE TOTALS

#	Account	Prior Week Total	Total for Week	Total to Date
Non-Deductible Expenses				
1	Inventory			
2	Equipment/Property			
3	Loans/Notes Paid			
4	Federal Income Tax			
5	Personal Expense			
6				
	Sub-Total			

#	Account	Prior Week Total	Total for Week	Total to Date
Deductible Expenses				
7	Advertising			
8	Auto/Truck/Travel			
9	Bank Fees			
10	Contributions			
11	Lodging			
12	Insurance			
13	Interest Paid			
14	Legal/Professional			
15	Meals/Entertainment			
16	Payroll (Net Pay)			
17	Payroll (Deductions)			
18	Postage/Freight			
19	Rent			
20	Repairs/Maintenance			
21	Taxes (Sales)			
22	Taxes (Other)			
23	Supplies/Tools			
24	Telephone/Internet			
25	Utilities			
26				
27				
	Sub-Total			

INCOME TOTALS

#	Account	Prior Week Total	Total for Week	Total to Date
1	Sale of Goods Income			
2	Service/Labor Income			
3	Miscellaneous Income			
4	Returns (deduct)	( )	( )	( )

Prior Week Total		
Total for Week		
Total to Date		

Prior Week Total		
Total for Week		
Total to Date		

WEEKLY EXPENSE AND INCOME RECORD

Week Ending On _____ , 20 _____

GENERAL EXPENSES

Date	Name and Description	Check # or Credit Card	Acct #	Amount	
	Total for Week				

INVENTORY EXPENSES

Date	Name and Description	Check # or Credit Card	Acct #	Amount	
			1		
			1		
			1		
			1		
			1		
			1		
			1		
			1		
			1		
			1		
			1		
			1		
	Total for Week				

EQUIPMENT/PROPERTY EXPENSES

Date	Name and Description	Check # or Credit Card	Acct #	Amount	
			2		
			2		
			2		
			2		
			2		
			2		
			2		
			2		
			2		
			2		
			2		
	Total for Week				

PAYROLL EXPENSES

Date	Employee	Check #	Acct #	Net Pay	
			16		
			16		
			16		
			16		
	Total for Week				

WEEKLY EXPENSE AND INCOME RECORD

Week Ending On _____ , 20 _____

WEEKLY INCOME OR RETURNS

Date	Name and Description	Check # or Cash	Acct #	Amount
	Total for Week			

EXPENSE TOTALS

#	Account	Prior Week Total	Total for Week	Total to Date
Non-Deductible Expenses				
1	Inventory			
2	Equipment/Property			
3	Loans/Notes Paid			
4	Federal Income Tax			
5	Personal Expense			
6				
	Sub-Total			

#	Account	Prior Week Total	Total for Week	Total to Date
Deductible Expenses				
7	Advertising			
8	Auto/Truck/Travel			
9	Bank Fees			
10	Contributions			
11	Lodging			
12	Insurance			
13	Interest Paid			
14	Legal/Professional			
15	Meals/Entertainment			
16	Payroll (Net Pay)			
17	Payroll (Deductions)			
18	Postage/Freight			
19	Rent			
20	Repairs/Maintenance			
21	Taxes (Sales)			
22	Taxes (Other)			
23	Supplies/Tools			
24	Telephone/Internet			
25	Utilities			
26				
27				
	Sub-Total			

INCOME TOTALS

#	Account	Prior Week Total	Total for Week	Total to Date
1	Sale of Goods Income			
2	Service/Labor Income			
3	Miscellaneous Income			
4	Returns (deduct)	( )	( )	( )

Prior Week Total	
Total for Week	
Total to Date	

Prior Week Total	
Total for Week	
Total to Date	

WEEKLY EXPENSE AND INCOME RECORD

Week Ending On _____ , 20 _____

GENERAL EXPENSES

Date	Name and Description	Check # or Credit Card	Acct #	Amount	
Total for Week					

INVENTORY EXPENSES

Date	Name and Description	Check # or Credit Card	Acct #	Amount	
			1		
			1		
			1		
			1		
			1		
			1		
			1		
			1		
			1		
			1		
			1		
			1		
Total for Week					

EQUIPMENT/PROPERTY EXPENSES

Date	Name and Description	Check # or Credit Card	Acct #	Amount	
			2		
			2		
			2		
			2		
			2		
			2		
			2		
			2		
			2		
			2		
			2		
Total for Week					

PAYROLL EXPENSES

Date	Employee	Check #	Acct #	Net Pay	
			16		
			16		
			16		
			16		
Total for Week					

WEEKLY EXPENSE AND INCOME RECORD

Week Ending On _____ , 20 ____

WEEKLY INCOME OR RETURNS

Date	Name and Description	Check # or Cash	Acct #	Amount	
	Total for Week				

EXPENSE TOTALS

#	Account	Prior Week Total	Total for Week	Total to Date
	Non Deductible Expenses			
1	Inventory			
2	Equipment/Property			
3	Loans/Notes Paid			
4	Federal Income Tax			
5	Personal Expense			
6				
	Sub-Total			

#	Account	Prior Week Total	Total for Week	Total to Date
	Deductible Expenses			
7	Advertising			
8	Auto/Truck/Travel			
9	Bank Fees			
10	Contributions			
11	Lodging			
12	Insurance			
13	Interest Paid			
14	Legal/Professional			
15	Meals/Entertainment			
16	Payroll (Net Pay)			
17	Payroll (Deductions)			
18	Postage/Freight			
19	Rent			
20	Repairs/Maintenance			
21	Taxes (Sales)			
22	Taxes (Other)			
23	Supplies/Tools			
24	Telephone/Internet			
25	Utilities			
26				
27				
	Sub-Total			

INCOME TOTALS

#	Account	Prior Week Total	Total for Week	Total to Date
1	Sale of Goods Income			
2	Service/Labor Income			
3	Miscellaneous Income			
4	Returns (deduct)	( )	( )	( )

Prior Week Total		
Total for Week		
Total to Date		

Prior Week Total		
Total for Week		
Total to Date		

WEEKLY EXPENSE AND INCOME RECORD

Week Ending On _____ , 20 ____

GENERAL EXPENSES

Date	Name and Description	Check # or Credit Card	Acct #	Amount
Total for Week				

INVENTORY EXPENSES

Date	Name and Description	Check # or Credit Card	Acct #	Amount
			1	
			1	
			1	
			1	
			1	
			1	
			1	
			1	
			1	
			1	
			1	
			1	
Total for Week				

EQUIPMENT/PROPERTY EXPENSES

Date	Name and Description	Check # or Credit Card	Acct #	Amount
			2	
			2	
			2	
			2	
			2	
			2	
			2	
			2	
			2	
			2	
			2	
Total for Week				

PAYROLL EXPENSES

Date	Employee	Check #	Acct #	Net Pay
			16	
			16	
			16	
			16	
Total for Week				

WEEKLY EXPENSE AND INCOME RECORD

Week Ending On _____ , 20 _____

WEEKLY INCOME OR RETURNS

Date	Name and Description	Check # or Cash	Acct #	Amount
Total for Week				

INCOME TOTALS

#	Account	Prior Week Total	Total for Week	Total to Date
1	Sale of Goods Income			
2	Service/Labor Income			
3	Miscellaneous Income			
4	Returns (deduct)	( )	( )	( )

Prior Week Total	
Total for Week	
Total to Date	

EXPENSE TOTALS

#	Account	Prior Week Total	Total for Week	Total to Date
	Non-Deductible Expenses			
1	Inventory			
2	Equipment/Property			
3	Loans/Notes Paid			
4	Federal Income Tax			
5	Personal Expense			
6				
	Sub-Total			

#	Account	Prior Week Total	Total for Week	Total to Date
	Deductible Expenses			
7	Advertising			
8	Auto/Truck/Travel			
9	Bank Fees			
10	Contributions			
11	Lodging			
12	Insurance			
13	Interest Paid			
14	Legal/Professional			
15	Meals/Entertainment			
16	Payroll (Net Pay)			
17	Payroll (Deductions)			
18	Postage/Freight			
19	Rent			
20	Repairs/Maintenance			
21	Taxes (Sales)			
22	Taxes (Other)			
23	Supplies/Tools			
24	Telephone/Internet			
25	Utilities			
26				
27				
	Sub-Total			

Prior Week Total	
Total for Week	
Total to Date	

WEEKLY EXPENSE AND INCOME RECORD

Week Ending On _____ , 20 _____

GENERAL EXPENSES

Date	Name and Description	Check # or Credit Card	Acct #	Amount	
Total for Week					

INVENTORY EXPENSES

Date	Name and Description	Check # or Credit Card	Acct #	Amount	
			1		
			1		
			1		
			1		
			1		
			1		
			1		
			1		
			1		
			1		
			1		
			1		
Total for Week					

EQUIPMENT/PROPERTY EXPENSES

Date	Name and Description	Check # or Credit Card	Acct #	Amount	
			2		
			2		
			2		
			2		
			2		
			2		
			2		
			2		
			2		
			2		
			2		
Total for Week					

PAYROLL EXPENSES

Date	Employee	Check #	Acct #	Net Pay	
			16		
			16		
			16		
			16		
Total for Week					

WEEKLY EXPENSE AND INCOME RECORD

Week Ending On _____ , 20 ____

WEEKLY INCOME OR RETURNS

Date	Name and Description	Check # or Cash	Acct #	Amount
	Total for Week			

EXPENSE TOTALS

#	Account	Prior Week Total	Total for Week	Total to Date
Non-Deductible Expenses				
1	Inventory			
2	Equipment/Property			
3	Loans/Notes Paid			
4	Federal Income Tax			
5	Personal Expense			
6				
	Sub-Total			

#	Account	Prior Week Total	Total for Week	Total to Date
Deductible Expenses				
7	Advertising			
8	Auto/Truck/Travel			
9	Bank Fees			
10	Contributions			
11	Lodging			
12	Insurance			
13	Interest Paid			
14	Legal/Professional			
15	Meals/Entertainment			
16	Payroll (Net Pay)			
17	Payroll (Deductions)			
18	Postage/Freight			
19	Rent			
20	Repairs/Maintenance			
21	Taxes (Sales)			
22	Taxes (Other)			
23	Supplies/Tools			
24	Telephone/Internet			
25	Utilities			
26				
27				
	Sub-Total			

INCOME TOTALS

#	Account	Prior Week Total	Total for Week	Total to Date
1	Sale of Goods Income			
2	Service/Labor Income			
3	Miscellaneous Income			
4	Returns (deduct)	( )	( )	( )

Prior Week Total		
Total for Week		
Total to Date		

Prior Week Total		
Total for Week		
Total to Date		

WEEKLY EXPENSE AND INCOME RECORD

Week Ending On _____ , 20 _____

GENERAL EXPENSES

Date	Name and Description	Check # or Credit Card	Acct #	Amount	
	Total for Week				

INVENTORY EXPENSES

Date	Name and Description	Check # or Credit Card	Acct #	Amount	
			1		
			1		
			1		
			1		
			1		
			1		
			1		
			1		
			1		
			1		
			1		
			1		
	Total for Week				

EQUIPMENT/PROPERTY EXPENSES

Date	Name and Description	Check # or Credit Card	Acct #	Amount	
			2		
			2		
			2		
			2		
			2		
			2		
			2		
			2		
			2		
			2		
	Total for Week				

PAYROLL EXPENSES

Date	Employee	Check #	Acct #	Net Pay	
			16		
			16		
			16		
			16		
	Total for Week				

WEEKLY EXPENSE AND INCOME RECORD

Week Ending On _____ , 20 _____

WEEKLY INCOME OR RETURNS

Date	Name and Description	Check # or Cash	Acct #	Amount	
Total for Week					

INCOME TOTALS

#	Account	Prior Week Total	Total for Week	Total to Date	
1	Sale of Goods Income				
2	Service/Labor Income				
3	Miscellaneous Income				
4	Returns (deduct)	( )	( )	( )	

	Prior Week Total		
Total for Week		
Total to Date		

EXPENSE TOTALS

#	Account	Prior Week Total		Total for Week		Total to Date	

Non-Deductible Expenses

1	Inventory						
2	Equipment/Property						
3	Loans/Notes Paid						
4	Federal Income Tax						
5	Personal Expense						
6							
	Sub-Total						

#	Account	Prior Week Total		Total for Week		Total to Date	

Deductible Expenses

7	Advertising						
8	Auto/Truck/Travel						
9	Bank Fees						
10	Contributions						
11	Lodging						
12	Insurance						
13	Interest Paid						
14	Legal/Professional						
15	Meals/Entertainment						
16	Payroll (Net Pay)						
17	Payroll (Deductions)						
18	Postage/Freight						
19	Rent						
20	Repairs/Maintenance						
21	Taxes (Sales)						
22	Taxes (Other)						
23	Supplies/Tools						
24	Telephone/Internet						
25	Utilities						
26							
27							
	Sub-Total						

	Prior Week Total		
Total for Week		
Total to Date		

WEEKLY EXPENSE AND INCOME RECORD

Week Ending On _____ , 20 _____

GENERAL EXPENSES

Date	Name and Description	Check # or Credit Card	Acct #	Amount	
		Total for Week			

INVENTORY EXPENSES

Date	Name and Description	Check # or Credit Card	Acct #	Amount	
			1		
			1		
			1		
			1		
			1		
			1		
			1		
			1		
			1		
			1		
			1		
			1		
		Total for Week			

EQUIPMENT/PROPERTY EXPENSES

Date	Name and Description	Check # or Credit Card	Acct #	Amount	
			2		
			2		
			2		
			2		
			2		
			2		
			2		
			2		
			2		
			2		
			2		
		Total for Week			

PAYROLL EXPENSES

Date	Employee	Check #	Acct #	Net Pay	
			16		
			16		
			16		
			16		
		Total for Week			

WEEKLY EXPENSE AND INCOME RECORD

Week Ending On _____ , 20 ____

WEEKLY INCOME OR RETURNS

Date	Name and Description	Check # or Cash	Acct #	Amount
Total for Week				

EXPENSE TOTALS

#	Account	Prior Week Total	Total for Week	Total to Date
Non-Deductible Expenses				
1	Inventory			
2	Equipment/Property			
3	Loans/Notes Paid			
4	Federal Income Tax			
5	Personal Expense			
6				
	Sub-Total			

#	Account	Prior Week Total	Total for Week	Total to Date
Deductible Expenses				
7	Advertising			
8	Auto/Truck/Travel			
9	Bank Fees			
10	Contributions			
11	Lodging			
12	Insurance			
13	Interest Paid			
14	Legal/Professional			
15	Meals/Entertainment			
16	Payroll (Net Pay)			
17	Payroll (Deductions)			
18	Postage/Freight			
19	Rent			
20	Repairs/Maintenance			
21	Taxes (Sales)			
22	Taxes (Other)			
23	Supplies/Tools			
24	Telephone/Internet			
25	Utilities			
26				
27				
	Sub-Total			

INCOME TOTALS

#	Account	Prior Week Total	Total for Week	Total to Date
1	Sale of Goods Income			
2	Service/Labor Income			
3	Miscellaneous Income			
4	Returns (deduct)	( )	( )	( )

Prior Week Total	
Total for Week	
Total to Date	

Prior Week Total	
Total for Week	
Total to Date	

WEEKLY EXPENSE AND INCOME RECORD

Week Ending On _____ , 20 ____

GENERAL EXPENSES

Date	Name and Description	Check # or Credit Card	Acct #	Amount	
	Total for Week				

INVENTORY EXPENSES

Date	Name and Description	Check # or Credit Card	Acct #	Amount	
			1		
			1		
			1		
			1		
			1		
			1		
			1		
			1		
			1		
			1		
			1		
			1		
	Total for Week				

EQUIPMENT/PROPERTY EXPENSES

Date	Name and Description	Check # or Credit Card	Acct #	Amount	
			2		
			2		
			2		
			2		
			2		
			2		
			2		
			2		
			2		
			2		
			2		
	Total for Week				

PAYROLL EXPENSES

Date	Employee	Check #	Acct #	Net Pay	
			16		
			16		
			16		
			16		
	Total for Week				

WEEKLY EXPENSE AND INCOME RECORD

Week Ending On _____ , 20 _____

WEEKLY INCOME OR RETURNS

Date	Name and Description	Check # or Cash	Acct #	Amount
	Total for Week			

EXPENSE TOTALS

#	Account	Prior Week Total	Total for Week	Total to Date
Non-Deductible Expenses				
1	Inventory			
2	Equipment/Property			
3	Loans/Notes Paid			
4	Federal Income Tax			
5	Personal Expense			
6				
	Sub-Total			

#	Account	Prior Week Total	Total for Week	Total to Date
Deductible Expenses				
7	Advertising			
8	Auto/Truck/Travel			
9	Bank Fees			
10	Contributions			
11	Lodging			
12	Insurance			
13	Interest Paid			
14	Legal/Professional			
15	Meals/Entertainment			
16	Payroll (Net Pay)			
17	Payroll (Deductions)			
18	Postage/Freight			
19	Rent			
20	Repairs/Maintenance			
21	Taxes (Sales)			
22	Taxes (Other)			
23	Supplies/Tools			
24	Telephone/Internet			
25	Utilities			
26				
27				
	Sub-Total			

INCOME TOTALS

#	Account	Prior Week Total	Total for Week	Total to Date
1	Sale of Goods Income			
2	Service/Labor Income			
3	Miscellaneous Income			
4	Returns (deduct)	( )	( )	( )

Prior Week Total		
Total for Week		
Total to Date		

Prior Week Total		
Total for Week		
Total to Date		

WEEKLY EXPENSE AND INCOME RECORD

Week Ending On _____ , 20 _____

GENERAL EXPENSES

Date	Name and Description	Check # or Credit Card	Acct #	Amount	
	Total for Week				

INVENTORY EXPENSES

Date	Name and Description	Check # or Credit Card	Acct #	Amount	
			1		
			1		
			1		
			1		
			1		
			1		
			1		
			1		
			1		
			1		
			1		
			1		
	Total for Week				

EQUIPMENT/PROPERTY EXPENSES

Date	Name and Description	Check # or Credit Card	Acct #	Amount	
			2		
			2		
			2		
			2		
			2		
			2		
			2		
			2		
			2		
			2		
			2		
	Total for Week				

PAYROLL EXPENSES

Date	Employee	Check #	Acct #	Net Pay	
			16		
			16		
			16		
			16		
	Total for Week				

WEEKLY EXPENSE AND INCOME RECORD

Week Ending On _____ , 20 _____

WEEKLY INCOME OR RETURNS

Date	Name and Description	Check # or Cash	Acct #	Amount
	Total for Week			

INCOME TOTALS

#	Account	Prior Week Total	Total for Week	Total to Date
1	Sale of Goods Income			
2	Service/Labor Income			
3	Miscellaneous Income			
4	Returns (deduct)	( )	( )	( )

Prior Week Total	
Total for Week	
Total to Date	

EXPENSE TOTALS

#	Account	Prior Week Total	Total for Week	Total to Date
Non-Deductible Expenses				
1	Inventory			
2	Equipment/Property			
3	Loans/Notes Paid			
4	Federal Income Tax			
5	Personal Expense			
6				
	Sub-Total			

#	Account	Prior Week Total	Total for Week	Total to Date
Deductible Expenses				
7	Advertising			
8	Auto/Truck/Travel			
9	Bank Fees			
10	Contributions			
11	Lodging			
12	Insurance			
13	Interest Paid			
14	Legal/Professional			
15	Meals/Entertainment			
16	Payroll (Net Pay)			
17	Payroll (Deductions)			
18	Postage/Freight			
19	Rent			
20	Repairs/Maintenance			
21	Taxes (Sales)			
22	Taxes (Other)			
23	Supplies/Tools			
24	Telephone/Internet			
25	Utilities			
26				
27				
	Sub-Total			

Prior Week Total	
Total for Week	
Total to Date	

WEEKLY EXPENSE AND INCOME RECORD

Week Ending On _____ , 20 ____

GENERAL EXPENSES

Date	Name and Description	Check # or Credit Card	Acct #	Amount	
	Total for Week				

INVENTORY EXPENSES

Date	Name and Description	Check # or Credit Card	Acct #	Amount	
			1		
			1		
			1		
			1		
			1		
			1		
			1		
			1		
			1		
			1		
			1		
			1		
	Total for Week				

EQUIPMENT/PROPERTY EXPENSES

Date	Name and Description	Check # or Credit Card	Acct #	Amount	
			2		
			2		
			2		
			2		
			2		
			2		
			2		
			2		
			2		
			2		
			2		
	Total for Week				

PAYROLL EXPENSES

Date	Employee	Check #	Acct #	Net Pay	
			16		
			16		
			16		
			16		
	Total for Week				

WEEKLY EXPENSE AND INCOME RECORD

Week Ending On _____ , 20 _____

WEEKLY INCOME OR RETURNS

Date	Name and Description	Check # or Cash	Acct #	Amount
Total for Week				

EXPENSE TOTALS

#	Account	Prior Week Total	Total for Week	Total to Date
Non-Deductible Expenses				
1	Inventory			
2	Equipment/Property			
3	Loans/Notes Paid			
4	Federal Income Tax			
5	Personal Expense			
6				
	Sub-Total			

#	Account	Prior Week Total	Total for Week	Total to Date
Deductible Expenses				
7	Advertising			
8	Auto/Truck/Travel			
9	Bank Fees			
10	Contributions			
11	Lodging			
12	Insurance			
13	Interest Paid			
14	Legal/Professional			
15	Meals/Entertainment			
16	Payroll (Net Pay)			
17	Payroll (Deductions)			
18	Postage/Freight			
19	Rent			
20	Repairs/Maintenance			
21	Taxes (Sales)			
22	Taxes (Other)			
23	Supplies/Tools			
24	Telephone/Internet			
25	Utilities			
26				
27				
	Sub-Total			

INCOME TOTALS

#	Account	Prior Week Total	Total for Week	Total to Date
1	Sale of Goods Income			
2	Service/Labor Income			
3	Miscellaneous Income			
4	Returns (deduct)	( )	( )	( )

Prior Week Total			
Total for Week			
Total to Date			

Prior Week Total			
Total for Week			
Total to Date			

WEEKLY EXPENSE AND INCOME RECORD

Week Ending On _____ , 20 _____

GENERAL EXPENSES

Date	Name and Description	Check # or Credit Card	Acct #	Amount
Total for Week				

INVENTORY EXPENSES

Date	Name and Description	Check # or Credit Card	Acct #	Amount
			1	
			1	
			1	
			1	
			1	
			1	
			1	
			1	
			1	
			1	
			1	
			1	
Total for Week				

EQUIPMENT/PROPERTY EXPENSES

Date	Name and Description	Check # or Credit Card	Acct #	Amount
			2	
			2	
			2	
			2	
			2	
			2	
			2	
			2	
			2	
			2	
			2	
Total for Week				

PAYROLL EXPENSES

Date	Employee	Check #	Acct #	Net Pay
			16	
			16	
			16	
			16	
Total for Week				

WEEKLY EXPENSE AND INCOME RECORD

Week Ending On _____ , 20 _____

WEEKLY INCOME OR RETURNS

Date	Name and Description	Check # or Cash	Acct #	Amount	
Total for Week					

INCOME TOTALS

#	Account	Prior Week Total	Total for Week	Total to Date	
1	Sale of Goods Income				
2	Service/Labor Income				
3	Miscellaneous Income				
4	Returns (deduct)	( )	( )	( )	

Prior Week Total		
Total for Week		
Total to Date		

EXPENSE TOTALS

#	Account	Prior Week Total	Total for Week	Total to Date	
	Non-Deductible Expenses				
1	Inventory				
2	Equipment/Property				
3	Loans/Notes Paid				
4	Federal Income Tax				
5	Personal Expense				
6					
	Sub-Total				

#	Account	Prior Week Total	Total for Week	Total to Date	
	Deductible Expenses				
7	Advertising				
8	Auto/Truck/Travel				
9	Bank Fees				
10	Contributions				
11	Lodging				
12	Insurance				
13	Interest Paid				
14	Legal/Professional				
15	Meals/Entertainment				
16	Payroll (Net Pay)				
17	Payroll (Deductions)				
18	Postage/Freight				
19	Rent				
20	Repairs/Maintenance				
21	Taxes (Sales)				
22	Taxes (Other)				
23	Supplies/Tools				
24	Telephone/Internet				
25	Utilities				
26					
27					
	Sub-Total				

Prior Week Total		
Total for Week		
Total to Date		

WEEKLY EXPENSE AND INCOME RECORD

Week Ending On _____ , 20 _____

GENERAL EXPENSES

Date	Name and Description	Check # or Credit Card	Acct #	Amount	
Total for Week					

INVENTORY EXPENSES

Date	Name and Description	Check # or Credit Card	Acct #	Amount	
			1		
			1		
			1		
			1		
			1		
			1		
			1		
			1		
			1		
			1		
			1		
			1		
Total for Week					

EQUIPMENT/PROPERTY EXPENSES

Date	Name and Description	Check # or Credit Card	Acct #	Amount	
			2		
			2		
			2		
			2		
			2		
			2		
			2		
			2		
			2		
			2		
			2		
Total for Week					

PAYROLL EXPENSES

Date	Employee	Check #	Acct #	Net Pay	
			16		
			16		
			16		
			16		
Total for Week					

WEEKLY EXPENSE AND INCOME RECORD

Week Ending On _____ , 20 _____

WEEKLY INCOME OR RETURNS

Date	Name and Description	Check # or Cash	Acct #	Amount
Total for Week				

EXPENSE TOTALS

#	Account	Prior Week Total	Total for Week	Total to Date
Non-Deductible Expenses				
1	Inventory			
2	Equipment/Property			
3	Loans/Notes Paid			
4	Federal Income Tax			
5	Personal Expense			
6				
	Sub-Total			

#	Account	Prior Week Total	Total for Week	Total to Date
Deductible Expenses				
7	Advertising			
8	Auto/Truck/Travel			
9	Bank Fees			
10	Contributions			
11	Lodging			
12	Insurance			
13	Interest Paid			
14	Legal/Professional			
15	Meals/Entertainment			
16	Payroll (Net Pay)			
17	Payroll (Deductions)			
18	Postage/Freight			
19	Rent			
20	Repairs/Maintenance			
21	Taxes (Sales)			
22	Taxes (Other)			
23	Supplies/Tools			
24	Telephone/Internet			
25	Utilities			
26				
27				
	Sub-Total			

INCOME TOTALS

#	Account	Prior Week Total	Total for Week	Total to Date
1	Sale of Goods Income			
2	Service/Labor Income			
3	Miscellaneous Income			
4	Returns (deduct)	( )	( )	( )

Prior Week Total	
Total for Week	
Total to Date	

Prior Week Total	
Total for Week	
Total to Date	

WEEKLY EXPENSE AND INCOME RECORD

Week Ending On _____ , 20 _____

GENERAL EXPENSES

Date	Name and Description	Check # or Credit Card	Acct #	Amount
	Total for Week			

INVENTORY EXPENSES

Date	Name and Description	Check # or Credit Card	Acct #	Amount
			1	
			1	
			1	
			1	
			1	
			1	
			1	
			1	
			1	
			1	
			1	
			1	
	Total for Week			

EQUIPMENT/PROPERTY EXPENSES

Date	Name and Description	Check # or Credit Card	Acct #	Amount
			2	
			2	
			2	
			2	
			2	
			2	
			2	
			2	
			2	
			2	
			2	
	Total for Week			

PAYROLL EXPENSES

Date	Employee	Check #	Acct #	Net Pay
			16	
			16	
			16	
			16	
	Total for Week			

WEEKLY EXPENSE AND INCOME RECORD

Week Ending On _____ , 20 ____

WEEKLY INCOME OR RETURNS

Date	Name and Description	Check # or Cash	Acct #	Amount
Total for Week				

EXPENSE TOTALS

#	Account	Prior Week Total	Total for Week	Total to Date
Non-Deductible Expenses				
1	Inventory			
2	Equipment/Property			
3	Loans/Notes Paid			
4	Federal Income Tax			
5	Personal Expense			
6				
	Sub-Total			

#	Account	Prior Week Total	Total for Week	Total to Date
Deductible Expenses				
7	Advertising			
8	Auto/Truck/Travel			
9	Bank Fees			
10	Contributions			
11	Lodging			
12	Insurance			
13	Interest Paid			
14	Legal/Professional			
15	Meals/Entertainment			
16	Payroll (Net Pay)			
17	Payroll (Deductions)			
18	Postage/Freight			
19	Rent			
20	Repairs/Maintenance			
21	Taxes (Sales)			
22	Taxes (Other)			
23	Supplies/Tools			
24	Telephone/Internet			
25	Utilities			
26				
27				
	Sub-Total			

INCOME TOTALS

#	Account	Prior Week Total	Total for Week	Total to Date
1	Sale of Goods Income			
2	Service/Labor Income			
3	Miscellaneous Income			
4	Returns (deduct)	( )	( )	( )
	Prior Week Total			
	Total for Week			
	Total to Date			

	Prior Week Total	
	Total for Week	
	Total to Date	

WEEKLY EXPENSE AND INCOME RECORD

Week Ending On _____ , 20 _____

GENERAL EXPENSES

Date	Name and Description	Check # or Credit Card	Acct #	Amount	
Total for Week					

INVENTORY EXPENSES

Date	Name and Description	Check # or Credit Card	Acct #	Amount	
			1		
			1		
			1		
			1		
			1		
			1		
			1		
			1		
			1		
			1		
			1		
			1		
Total for Week					

EQUIPMENT/PROPERTY EXPENSES

Date	Name and Description	Check # or Credit Card	Acct #	Amount	
			2		
			2		
			2		
			2		
			2		
			2		
			2		
			2		
			2		
			2		
			2		
Total for Week					

PAYROLL EXPENSES

Date	Employee	Check #	Acct #	Net Pay	
			16		
			16		
			16		
			16		
Total for Week					

WEEKLY EXPENSE AND INCOME RECORD

Week Ending On _____ , 20 _____

WEEKLY INCOME OR RETURNS

Date	Name and Description	Check # or Cash	Acct #	Amount
	Total for Week			

EXPENSE TOTALS

#	Account	Prior Week Total	Total for Week	Total to Date
Non-Deductible Expenses				
1	Inventory			
2	Equipment/Property			
3	Loans/Notes Paid			
4	Federal Income Tax			
5	Personal Expense			
6				
	Sub-Total			

#	Account	Prior Week Total	Total for Week	Total to Date
Deductible Expenses				
7	Advertising			
8	Auto/Truck/Travel			
9	Bank Fees			
10	Contributions			
11	Lodging			
12	Insurance			
13	Interest Paid			
14	Legal/Professional			
15	Meals/Entertainment			
16	Payroll (Net Pay)			
17	Payroll (Deductions)			
18	Postage/Freight			
19	Rent			
20	Repairs/Maintenance			
21	Taxes (Sales)			
22	Taxes (Other)			
23	Supplies/Tools			
24	Telephone/Internet			
25	Utilities			
26				
27				
	Sub-Total			

INCOME TOTALS

#	Account	Prior Week Total	Total for Week	Total to Date
1	Sale of Goods Income			
2	Service/Labor Income			
3	Miscellaneous Income			
4	Returns (deduct)	( )	( )	( )

Prior Week Total	
Total for Week	
Total to Date	

Prior Week Total	
Total for Week	
Total to Date	

WEEKLY EXPENSE AND INCOME RECORD

Week Ending On _____ , 20 _____

GENERAL EXPENSES

Date	Name and Description	Check # or Credit Card	Acct #	Amount	
Total for Week					

INVENTORY EXPENSES

Date	Name and Description	Check # or Credit Card	Acct #	Amount	
			1		
			1		
			1		
			1		
			1		
			1		
			1		
			1		
			1		
			1		
			1		
			1		
Total for Week					

EQUIPMENT/PROPERTY EXPENSES

Date	Name and Description	Check # or Credit Card	Acct #	Amount	
			2		
			2		
			2		
			2		
			2		
			2		
			2		
			2		
			2		
			2		
			2		
Total for Week					

PAYROLL EXPENSES

Date	Employee	Check #	Acct #	Net Pay	
			16		
			16		
			16		
			16		
Total for Week					

WEEKLY EXPENSE AND INCOME RECORD

Week Ending On _____ , 20 _____

WEEKLY INCOME OR RETURNS

Date	Name and Description	Check # or Cash	Acct #	Amount	
	Total for Week				

EXPENSE TOTALS

#	Account	Prior Week Total	Total for Week	Total to Date	
Non-Deductible Expenses					
1	Inventory				
2	Equipment/Property				
3	Loans/Notes Paid				
4	Federal Income Tax				
5	Personal Expense				
6					
	Sub-Total				

#	Account	Prior Week Total	Total for Week	Total to Date	
Deductible Expenses					
7	Advertising				
8	Auto/Truck/Travel				
9	Bank Fees				
10	Contributions				
11	Lodging				
12	Insurance				
13	Interest Paid				
14	Legal/Professional				
15	Meals/Entertainment				
16	Payroll (Net Pay)				
17	Payroll (Deductions)				
18	Postage/Freight				
19	Rent				
20	Repairs/Maintenance				
21	Taxes (Sales)				
22	Taxes (Other)				
23	Supplies/Tools				
24	Telephone/Internet				
25	Utilities				
26					
27					
	Sub-Total				

INCOME TOTALS

#	Account	Prior Week Total	Total for Week	Total to Date	
1	Sale of Goods Income				
2	Service/Labor Income				
3	Miscellaneous Income				
4	Returns (deduct)	( )	( )	( )	
	Prior Week Total				
	Total for Week				
	Total to Date				

Prior Week Total			
Total for Week			
Total to Date			

WEEKLY EXPENSE AND INCOME RECORD

Week Ending On _____ , 20 _____

GENERAL EXPENSES

Date	Name and Description	Check # or Credit Card	Acct #	Amount	
		Total for Week			

INVENTORY EXPENSES

Date	Name and Description	Check # or Credit Card	Acct #	Amount	
			1		
			1		
			1		
			1		
			1		
			1		
			1		
			1		
			1		
			1		
			1		
		Total for Week			

EQUIPMENT/PROPERTY EXPENSES

Date	Name and Description	Check # or Credit Card	Acct #	Amount	
			2		
			2		
			2		
			2		
			2		
			2		
			2		
			2		
			2		
			2		
			2		
		Total for Week			

PAYROLL EXPENSES

Date	Employee	Check #	Acct #	Net Pay	
			16		
			16		
			16		
			16		
		Total for Week			

WEEKLY EXPENSE AND INCOME RECORD

Week Ending On _____ , 20 ____

WEEKLY INCOME OR RETURNS

Date	Name and Description	Check # or Cash	Acct #	Amount	
Total for Week					

EXPENSE TOTALS

#	Account	Prior Week Total	Total for Week	Total to Date
Non-Deductible Expenses				
1	Inventory			
2	Equipment/Property			
3	Loans/Notes Paid			
4	Federal Income Tax			
5	Personal Expense			
6				
	Sub-Total			

#	Account	Prior Week Total	Total for Week	Total to Date
Deductible Expenses				
7	Advertising			
8	Auto/Truck/Travel			
9	Bank Fees			
10	Contributions			
11	Lodging			
12	Insurance			
13	Interest Paid			
14	Legal/Professional			
15	Meals/Entertainment			
16	Payroll (Net Pay)			
17	Payroll (Deductions)			
18	Postage/Freight			
19	Rent			
20	Repairs/Maintenance			
21	Taxes (Sales)			
22	Taxes (Other)			
23	Supplies/Tools			
24	Telephone/Internet			
25	Utilities			
26				
27				
	Sub-Total			

INCOME TOTALS

#	Account	Prior Week Total	Total for Week	Total to Date
1	Sale of Goods Income			
2	Service/Labor Income			
3	Miscellaneous Income			
4	Returns (deduct)	( )	( )	( )
	Prior Week Total			
	Total for Week			
	Total to Date			

Prior Week Total	
Total for Week	
Total to Date	

WEEKLY EXPENSE AND INCOME RECORD

Week Ending On _____ , 20 _____

GENERAL EXPENSES

Date	Name and Description	Check # or Credit Card	Acct #	Amount	
Total for Week					

INVENTORY EXPENSES

Date	Name and Description	Check # or Credit Card	Acct #	Amount	
			1		
			1		
			1		
			1		
			1		
			1		
			1		
			1		
			1		
			1		
			1		
			1		
Total for Week					

EQUIPMENT/PROPERTY EXPENSES

Date	Name and Description	Check # or Credit Card	Acct #	Amount	
			2		
			2		
			2		
			2		
			2		
			2		
			2		
			2		
			2		
			2		
			2		
Total for Week					

PAYROLL EXPENSES

Date	Employee	Check #	Acct #	Net Pay	
			16		
			16		
			16		
			16		
Total for Week					

WEEKLY EXPENSE AND INCOME RECORD

Week Ending On _____ , 20 ____

WEEKLY INCOME OR RETURNS

Date	Name and Description	Check # or Cash	Acct #	Amount
Total for Week				

INCOME TOTALS

#	Account	Prior Week Total	Total for Week	Total to Date
1	Sale of Goods Income			
2	Service/Labor Income			
3	Miscellaneous Income			
4	Returns (deduct)	( )	( )	( )
Prior Week Total				
Total for Week				
Total to Date				

EXPENSE TOTALS

#	Account	Prior Week Total	Total for Week	Total to Date
	Non-Deductible Expenses			
1	Inventory			
2	Equipment/Property			
3	Loans/Notes Paid			
4	Federal Income Tax			
5	Personal Expense			
6				
	Sub-Total			

#	Account	Prior Week Total	Total for Week	Total to Date
	Deductible Expenses			
7	Advertising			
8	Auto/Truck/Travel			
9	Bank Fees			
10	Contributions			
11	Lodging			
12	Insurance			
13	Interest Paid			
14	Legal/Professional			
15	Meals/Entertainment			
16	Payroll (Net Pay)			
17	Payroll (Deductions)			
18	Postage/Freight			
19	Rent			
20	Repairs/Maintenance			
21	Taxes (Sales)			
22	Taxes (Other)			
23	Supplies/Tools			
24	Telephone/Internet			
25	Utilities			
26				
27				
	Sub-Total			
Prior Week Total				
Total for Week				
Total to Date				

WEEKLY EXPENSE AND INCOME RECORD

Week Ending On _____ , 20 ____

GENERAL EXPENSES

Date	Name and Description	Check # or Credit Card	Acct #	Amount	
	Total for Week				

INVENTORY EXPENSES

Date	Name and Description	Check # or Credit Card	Acct #	Amount	
			1		
			1		
			1		
			1		
			1		
			1		
			1		
			1		
			1		
			1		
			1		
	Total for Week				

EQUIPMENT/PROPERTY EXPENSES

Date	Name and Description	Check # or Credit Card	Acct #	Amount	
			2		
			2		
			2		
			2		
			2		
			2		
			2		
			2		
			2		
			2		
			2		
	Total for Week				

PAYROLL EXPENSES

Date	Employee	Check #	Acct #	Net Pay	
			16		
			16		
			16		
			16		
	Total for Week				

WEEKLY EXPENSE AND INCOME RECORD

Week Ending On _____ , 20 _____

WEEKLY INCOME OR RETURNS

Date	Name and Description	Check # or Cash	Acct #	Amount
	Total for Week			

EXPENSE TOTALS

#	Account	Prior Week Total	Total for Week	Total to Date
Non-Deductible Expenses				
1	Inventory			
2	Equipment/Property			
3	Loans/Notes Paid			
4	Federal Income Tax			
5	Personal Expense			
6				
	Sub-Total			

#	Account	Prior Week Total	Total for Week	Total to Date
Deductible Expenses				
7	Advertising			
8	Auto/Truck/Travel			
9	Bank Fees			
10	Contributions			
11	Lodging			
12	Insurance			
13	Interest Paid			
14	Legal/Professional			
15	Meals/Entertainment			
16	Payroll (Net Pay)			
17	Payroll (Deductions)			
18	Postage/Freight			
19	Rent			
20	Repairs/Maintenance			
21	Taxes (Sales)			
22	Taxes (Other)			
23	Supplies/Tools			
24	Telephone/Internet			
25	Utilities			
26				
27				
	Sub-Total			

INCOME TOTALS

#	Account	Prior Week Total	Total for Week	Total to Date
1	Sale of Goods Income			
2	Service/Labor Income			
3	Miscellaneous Income			
4	Returns (deduct)	( )	( )	( )

Prior Week Total		
Total for Week		
Total to Date		

Prior Week Total		
Total for Week		
Total to Date		

WEEKLY EXPENSE AND INCOME RECORD

Week Ending On _____ , 20 _____

GENERAL EXPENSES

Date	Name and Description	Check # or Credit Card	Acct #	Amount	
	Total for Week				

INVENTORY EXPENSES

Date	Name and Description	Check # or Credit Card	Acct #	Amount	
			1		
			1		
			1		
			1		
			1		
			1		
			1		
			1		
			1		
			1		
			1		
			1		
	Total for Week				

EQUIPMENT/PROPERTY EXPENSES

Date	Name and Description	Check # or Credit Card	Acct #	Amount	
			2		
			2		
			2		
			2		
			2		
			2		
			2		
			2		
			2		
			2		
	Total for Week				

PAYROLL EXPENSES

Date	Employee	Check #	Acct #	Net Pay	
			16		
			16		
			16		
			16		
	Total for Week				

WEEKLY EXPENSE AND INCOME RECORD

Week Ending On _____ , 20 _____

WEEKLY INCOME OR RETURNS

Date	Name and Description	Check # or Cash	Acct #	Amount
	Total for Week			

INCOME TOTALS

#	Account	Prior Week Total	Total for Week	Total to Date
1	Sale of Goods Income			
2	Service/Labor Income			
3	Miscellaneous Income			
4	Returns (deduct)	( )	( )	( )

Prior Week Total	
Total for Week	
Total to Date	

EXPENSE TOTALS

#	Account	Prior Week Total	Total for Week	Total to Date
Non Deductible Expenses				
1	Inventory			
2	Equipment/Property			
3	Loans/Notes Paid			
4	Federal Income Tax			
5	Personal Expense			
6				
	Sub-Total			

#	Account	Prior Week Total	Total for Week	Total to Date
Deductible Expenses				
7	Advertising			
8	Auto/Truck/Travel			
9	Bank Fees			
10	Contributions			
11	Lodging			
12	Insurance			
13	Interest Paid			
14	Legal/Professional			
15	Meals/Entertainment			
16	Payroll (Net Pay)			
17	Payroll (Deductions)			
18	Postage/Freight			
19	Rent			
20	Repairs/Maintenance			
21	Taxes (Sales)			
22	Taxes (Other)			
23	Supplies/Tools			
24	Telephone/Internet			
25	Utilities			
26				
27				
	Sub-Total			

Prior Week Total	
Total for Week	
Total to Date	

WEEKLY EXPENSE AND INCOME RECORD

Week Ending On _____ , 20 _____

GENERAL EXPENSES

Date	Name and Description	Check # or Credit Card	Acct #	Amount	
	Total for Week				

INVENTORY EXPENSES

Date	Name and Description	Check # or Credit Card	Acct #	Amount	
			1		
			1		
			1		
			1		
			1		
			1		
			1		
			1		
			1		
			1		
			1		
			1		
	Total for Week				

EQUIPMENT/PROPERTY EXPENSES

Date	Name and Description	Check # or Credit Card	Acct #	Amount	
			2		
			2		
			2		
			2		
			2		
			2		
			2		
			2		
			2		
			2		
			2		
	Total for Week				

PAYROLL EXPENSES

Date	Employee	Check #	Acct #	Net Pay	
			16		
			16		
			16		
			16		
	Total for Week				

WEEKLY EXPENSE AND INCOME RECORD

Week Ending On _____ , 20 _____

WEEKLY INCOME OR RETURNS

Date	Name and Description	Check # or Cash	Acct #	Amount
		Total for Week		

EXPENSE TOTALS

#	Account	Prior Week Total	Total for Week	Total to Date
Non-Deductible Expenses				
1	Inventory			
2	Equipment/Property			
3	Loans/Notes Paid			
4	Federal Income Tax			
5	Personal Expense			
6				
	Sub-Total			

#	Account	Prior Week Total	Total for Week	Total to Date
Deductible Expenses				
7	Advertising			
8	Auto/Truck/Travel			
9	Bank Fees			
10	Contributions			
11	Lodging			
12	Insurance			
13	Interest Paid			
14	Legal/Professional			
15	Meals/Entertainment			
16	Payroll (Net Pay)			
17	Payroll (Deductions)			
18	Postage/Freight			
19	Rent			
20	Repairs/Maintenance			
21	Taxes (Sales)			
22	Taxes (Other)			
23	Supplies/Tools			
24	Telephone/Internet			
25	Utilities			
26				
27				
	Sub-Total			

INCOME TOTALS

#	Account	Prior Week Total	Total for Week	Total to Date
1	Sale of Goods Income			
2	Service/Labor Income			
3	Miscellaneous Income			
4	Returns (deduct)	( )	( )	( )

Prior Week Total	
Total for Week	
Total to Date	

Prior Week Total	
Total for Week	
Total to Date	

WEEKLY EXPENSE AND INCOME RECORD

Week Ending On _____ , 20 _____

GENERAL EXPENSES

Date	Name and Description	Check # or Credit Card	Acct #	Amount	
	Total for Week				

INVENTORY EXPENSES

Date	Name and Description	Check # or Credit Card	Acct #	Amount	
			1		
			1		
			1		
			1		
			1		
			1		
			1		
			1		
			1		
			1		
			1		
			1		
	Total for Week				

EQUIPMENT/PROPERTY EXPENSES

Date	Name and Description	Check # or Credit Card	Acct #	Amount	
			2		
			2		
			2		
			2		
			2		
			2		
			2		
			2		
			2		
			2		
			2		
	Total for Week				

PAYROLL EXPENSES

Date	Employee	Check #	Acct #	Net Pay	
			16		
			16		
			16		
			16		
	Total for Week				

WEEKLY EXPENSE AND INCOME RECORD

Week Ending On _____ , 20 ____

WEEKLY INCOME OR RETURNS

Date	Name and Description	Check # or Cash	Acct #	Amount	
Total for Week					

INCOME TOTALS

#	Account	Prior Week Total		Total for Week		Total to Date	
1	Sale of Goods Income						
2	Service/Labor Income						
3	Miscellaneous Income						
4	Returns (deduct)	(	)	(	)	(	)

Prior Week Total		
Total for Week		
Total to Date		

EXPENSE TOTALS

#	Account	Prior Week Total		Total for Week		Total to Date	
Non-Deductible Expenses							
1	Inventory						
2	Equipment/Property						
3	Loans/Notes Paid						
4	Federal Income Tax						
5	Personal Expense						
6							
	Sub-Total						

#	Account	Prior Week Total		Total for Week		Total to Date	
Deductible Expenses							
7	Advertising						
8	Auto/Truck/Travel						
9	Bank Fees						
10	Contributions						
11	Lodging						
12	Insurance						
13	Interest Paid						
14	Legal/Professional						
15	Meals/Entertainment						
16	Payroll (Net Pay)						
17	Payroll (Deductions)						
18	Postage/Freight						
19	Rent						
20	Repairs/Maintenance						
21	Taxes (Sales)						
22	Taxes (Other)						
23	Supplies/Tools						
24	Telephone/Internet						
25	Utilities						
26							
27							
	Sub-Total						

Prior Week Total		
Total for Week		
Total to Date		

WEEKLY EXPENSE AND INCOME RECORD

Week Ending On _____ , 20 _____

GENERAL EXPENSES

Date	Name and Description	Check # or Credit Card	Acct #	Amount	
Total for Week					

INVENTORY EXPENSES

Date	Name and Description	Check # or Credit Card	Acct #	Amount	
			1		
			1		
			1		
			1		
			1		
			1		
			1		
			1		
			1		
			1		
			1		
			1		
Total for Week					

EQUIPMENT/PROPERTY EXPENSES

Date	Name and Description	Check # or Credit Card	Acct #	Amount	
			2		
			2		
			2		
			2		
			2		
			2		
			2		
			2		
			2		
			2		
			2		
Total for Week					

PAYROLL EXPENSES

Date	Employee	Check #	Acct #	Net Pay	
			16		
			16		
			16		
			16		
Total for Week					

WEEKLY EXPENSE AND INCOME RECORD

Week Ending On _____ , 20 _____

WEEKLY INCOME OR RETURNS

Date	Name and Description	Check # or Cash	Acct #	Amount
	Total for Week			

INCOME TOTALS

#	Account	Prior Week Total	Total for Week	Total to Date
1	Sale of Goods Income			
2	Service/Labor Income			
3	Miscellaneous Income			
4	Returns (deduct)	( )	( )	( )
	Prior Week Total			
	Total for Week			
	Total to Date			

EXPENSE TOTALS

#	Account	Prior Week Total	Total for Week	Total to Date
Non-Deductible Expenses				
1	Inventory			
2	Equipment/Property			
3	Loans/Notes Paid			
4	Federal Income Tax			
5	Personal Expense			
6				
	Sub-Total			

#	Account	Prior Week Total	Total for Week	Total to Date
Deductible Expenses				
7	Advertising			
8	Auto/Truck/Travel			
9	Bank Fees			
10	Contributions			
11	Lodging			
12	Insurance			
13	Interest Paid			
14	Legal/Professional			
15	Meals/Entertainment			
16	Payroll (Net Pay)			
17	Payroll (Deductions)			
18	Postage/Freight			
19	Rent			
20	Repairs/Maintenance			
21	Taxes (Sales)			
22	Taxes (Other)			
23	Supplies/Tools			
24	Telephone/Internet			
25	Utilities			
26				
27				
	Sub-Total			
	Prior Week Total			
	Total for Week			
	Total to Date			

WEEKLY EXPENSE AND INCOME RECORD

Week Ending On _____ , 20 _____

GENERAL EXPENSES

Date	Name and Description	Check # or Credit Card	Acct #	Amount	
Total for Week					

INVENTORY EXPENSES

Date	Name and Description	Check # or Credit Card	Acct #	Amount	
			1		
			1		
			1		
			1		
			1		
			1		
			1		
			1		
			1		
			1		
			1		
			1		
Total for Week					

EQUIPMENT/PROPERTY EXPENSES

Date	Name and Description	Check # or Credit Card	Acct #	Amount	
			2		
			2		
			2		
			2		
			2		
			2		
			2		
			2		
			2		
			2		
			2		
Total for Week					

PAYROLL EXPENSES

Date	Employee	Check #	Acct #	Net Pay	
			16		
			16		
			16		
			16		
Total for Week					

WEEKLY EXPENSE AND INCOME RECORD

Week Ending On _____ , 20 _____

WEEKLY INCOME OR RETURNS

Date	Name and Description	Check # or Cash	Acct #	Amount
	Total for Week			

EXPENSE TOTALS

#	Account	Prior Week Total	Total for Week	Total to Date
Non-Deductible Expenses				
1	Inventory			
2	Equipment/Property			
3	Loans/Notes Paid			
4	Federal Income Tax			
5	Personal Expense			
6				
	Sub-Total			

#	Account	Prior Week Total	Total for Week	Total to Date
Deductible Expenses				
7	Advertising			
8	Auto/Truck/Travel			
9	Bank Fees			
10	Contributions			
11	Lodging			
12	Insurance			
13	Interest Paid			
14	Legal/Professional			
15	Meals/Entertainment			
16	Payroll (Net Pay)			
17	Payroll (Deductions)			
18	Postage/Freight			
19	Rent			
20	Repairs/Maintenance			
21	Taxes (Sales)			
22	Taxes (Other)			
23	Supplies/Tools			
24	Telephone/Internet			
25	Utilities			
26				
27				
	Sub-Total			

INCOME TOTALS

#	Account	Prior Week Total	Total for Week	Total to Date
1	Sale of Goods Income			
2	Service/Labor Income			
3	Miscellaneous Income			
4	Returns (deduct)	( )	( )	( )

Prior Week Total	
Total for Week	
Total to Date	

Prior Week Total	
Total for Week	
Total to Date	

WEEKLY EXPENSE AND INCOME RECORD

Week Ending On _____ , 20 ____

GENERAL EXPENSES

Date	Name and Description	Check # or Credit Card	Acct #	Amount	
Total for Week					

INVENTORY EXPENSES

Date	Name and Description	Check # or Credit Card	Acct #	Amount	
			1		
			1		
			1		
			1		
			1		
			1		
			1		
			1		
			1		
			1		
			1		
			1		
Total for Week					

EQUIPMENT/PROPERTY EXPENSES

Date	Name and Description	Check # or Credit Card	Acct #	Amount	
			2		
			2		
			2		
			2		
			2		
			2		
			2		
			2		
			2		
			2		
			2		
Total for Week					

PAYROLL EXPENSES

Date	Employee	Check #	Acct #	Net Pay	
			16		
			16		
			16		
			16		
Total for Week					

WEEKLY EXPENSE AND INCOME RECORD

Week Ending On _____ , 20 _____

WEEKLY INCOME OR RETURNS

Date	Name and Description	Check # or Cash	Acct #	Amount	
	Total for Week				

EXPENSE TOTALS

#	Account	Prior Week Total	Total for Week	Total to Date	
Non Deductible Expenses					
1	Inventory				
2	Equipment/Property				
3	Loans/Notes Paid				
4	Federal Income Tax				
5	Personal Expense				
6					
	Sub-Total				

#	Account	Prior Week Total	Total for Week	Total to Date	
Deductible Expenses					
7	Advertising				
8	Auto/Truck/Travel				
9	Bank Fees				
10	Contributions				
11	Lodging				
12	Insurance				
13	Interest Paid				
14	Legal/Professional				
15	Meals/Entertainment				
16	Payroll (Net Pay)				
17	Payroll (Deductions)				
18	Postage/Freight				
19	Rent				
20	Repairs/Maintenance				
21	Taxes (Sales)				
22	Taxes (Other)				
23	Supplies/Tools				
24	Telephone/Internet				
25	Utilities				
26					
27					
	Sub-Total				

INCOME TOTALS

#	Account	Prior Week Total	Total for Week	Total to Date	
1	Sale of Goods Income				
2	Service/Labor Income				
3	Miscellaneous Income				
4	Returns (deduct)	( )	( )	( )	

Prior Week Total			
Total for Week			
Total to Date			

Prior Week Total			
Total for Week			
Total to Date			

WEEKLY EXPENSE AND INCOME RECORD

Week Ending On _____ , 20 _____

GENERAL EXPENSES

Date	Name and Description	Check # or Credit Card	Acct #	Amount	
Total for Week					

INVENTORY EXPENSES

Date	Name and Description	Check # or Credit Card	Acct #	Amount	
			1		
			1		
			1		
			1		
			1		
			1		
			1		
			1		
			1		
			1		
			1		
			1		
Total for Week					

EQUIPMENT/PROPERTY EXPENSES

Date	Name and Description	Check # or Credit Card	Acct #	Amount	
			2		
			2		
			2		
			2		
			2		
			2		
			2		
			2		
			2		
			2		
			2		
Total for Week					

PAYROLL EXPENSES

Date	Employee	Check #	Acct #	Net Pay	
			16		
			16		
			16		
			16		
Total for Week					

WEEKLY EXPENSE AND INCOME RECORD

Week Ending On _____ , 20 ____

WEEKLY INCOME OR RETURNS

Date	Name and Description	Check # or Cash	Acct #	Amount	
	Total for Week				

INCOME TOTALS

#	Account	Prior Week Total	Total for Week	Total to Date	
1	Sale of Goods Income				
2	Service/Labor Income				
3	Miscellaneous Income				
4	Returns (deduct)	( )	( )	( )	

Prior Week Total		
Total for Week		
Total to Date		

EXPENSE TOTALS

#	Account	Prior Week Total	Total for Week	Total to Date	
	Non-Deductible Expenses				
1	Inventory				
2	Equipment/Property				
3	Loans/Notes Paid				
4	Federal Income Tax				
5	Personal Expense				
6					
	Sub-Total				

#	Account	Prior Week Total	Total for Week	Total to Date	
	Deductible Expenses				
7	Advertising				
8	Auto/Truck/Travel				
9	Bank Fees				
10	Contributions				
11	Lodging				
12	Insurance				
13	Interest Paid				
14	Legal/Professional				
15	Meals/Entertainment				
16	Payroll (Net Pay)				
17	Payroll (Deductions)				
18	Postage/Freight				
19	Rent				
20	Repairs/Maintenance				
21	Taxes (Sales)				
22	Taxes (Other)				
23	Supplies/Tools				
24	Telephone/Internet				
25	Utilities				
26					
27					
	Sub-Total				

Prior Week Total		
Total for Week		
Total to Date		

WEEKLY EXPENSE AND INCOME RECORD

Week Ending On _____ , 20 _____

GENERAL EXPENSES

Date	Name and Description	Check # or Credit Card	Acct #	Amount	
Total for Week					

INVENTORY EXPENSES

Date	Name and Description	Check # or Credit Card	Acct #	Amount	
			1		
			1		
			1		
			1		
			1		
			1		
			1		
			1		
			1		
			1		
			1		
			1		
Total for Week					

EQUIPMENT/PROPERTY EXPENSES

Date	Name and Description	Check # or Credit Card	Acct #	Amount	
			2		
			2		
			2		
			2		
			2		
			2		
			2		
			2		
			2		
			2		
			2		
Total for Week					

PAYROLL EXPENSES

Date	Employee	Check #	Acct #	Net Pay	
			16		
			16		
			16		
			16		
Total for Week					

WEEKLY EXPENSE AND INCOME RECORD

Week Ending On _____ , 20 _____

WEEKLY INCOME OR RETURNS

Date	Name and Description	Check # or Cash	Acct #	Amount	
Total for Week					

INCOME TOTALS

#	Account	Prior Week Total	Total for Week	Total to Date	
1	Sale of Goods Income				
2	Service/Labor Income				
3	Miscellaneous Income				
4	Returns (deduct)	( )	( )	( )	

Prior Week Total			
Total for Week			
Total to Date			

EXPENSE TOTALS

#	Account	Prior Week Total	Total for Week	Total to Date	
	Non-Deductible Expenses				
1	Inventory				
2	Equipment/Property				
3	Loans/Notes Paid				
4	Federal Income Tax				
5	Personal Expense				
6					
	Sub-Total				

#	Account	Prior Week Total	Total for Week	Total to Date	
	Deductible Expenses				
7	Advertising				
8	Auto/Truck/Travel				
9	Bank Fees				
10	Contributions				
11	Lodging				
12	Insurance				
13	Interest Paid				
14	Legal/Professional				
15	Meals/Entertainment				
16	Payroll (Net Pay)				
17	Payroll (Deductions)				
18	Postage/Freight				
19	Rent				
20	Repairs/Maintenance				
21	Taxes (Sales)				
22	Taxes (Other)				
23	Supplies/Tools				
24	Telephone/Internet				
25	Utilities				
26					
27					
	Sub-Total				

Prior Week Total			
Total for Week			
Total to Date			

WEEKLY EXPENSE AND INCOME RECORD

Week Ending On _____ , 20 ____

GENERAL EXPENSES

Date	Name and Description	Check # or Credit Card	Acct #	Amount	
	Total for Week				

INVENTORY EXPENSES

Date	Name and Description	Check # or Credit Card	Acct #	Amount	
			1		
			1		
			1		
			1		
			1		
			1		
			1		
			1		
			1		
			1		
			1		
			1		
	Total for Week				

EQUIPMENT/PROPERTY EXPENSES

Date	Name and Description	Check # or Credit Card	Acct #	Amount	
			2		
			2		
			2		
			2		
			2		
			2		
			2		
			2		
			2		
			2		
			2		
	Total for Week				

PAYROLL EXPENSES

Date	Employee	Check #	Acct #	Net Pay	
			16		
			16		
			16		
			16		
	Total for Week				

WEEKLY EXPENSE AND INCOME RECORD

Week Ending On _____ , 20 _____

WEEKLY INCOME OR RETURNS

Date	Name and Description	Check # or Cash	Acct #	Amount
	Total for Week			

INCOME TOTALS

#	Account	Prior Week Total	Total for Week	Total to Date
1	Sale of Goods Income			
2	Service/Labor Income			
3	Miscellaneous Income			
4	Returns (deduct)	( )	( )	( )

Prior Week Total	
Total for Week	
Total to Date	

EXPENSE TOTALS

#	Account	Prior Week Total	Total for Week	Total to Date
Non Deductible Expenses				
1	Inventory			
2	Equipment/Property			
3	Loans/Notes Paid			
4	Federal Income Tax			
5	Personal Expense			
6				
	Sub-Total			

#	Account	Prior Week Total	Total for Week	Total to Date
Deductible Expenses				
7	Advertising			
8	Auto/Truck/Travel			
9	Bank Fees			
10	Contributions			
11	Lodging			
12	Insurance			
13	Interest Paid			
14	Legal/Professional			
15	Meals/Entertainment			
16	Payroll (Net Pay)			
17	Payroll (Deductions)			
18	Postage/Freight			
19	Rent			
20	Repairs/Maintenance			
21	Taxes (Sales)			
22	Taxes (Other)			
23	Supplies/Tools			
24	Telephone/Internet			
25	Utilities			
26				
27				
	Sub-Total			

Prior Week Total	
Total for Week	
Total to Date	

WEEKLY EXPENSE AND INCOME RECORD

Week Ending On _____ , 20 _____

GENERAL EXPENSES				
Date	Name and Description	Check # or Credit Card	Acct #	Amount
Total for Week				

INVENTORY EXPENSES				
Date	Name and Description	Check # or Credit Card	Acct #	Amount
			1	
			1	
			1	
			1	
			1	
			1	
			1	
			1	
			1	
			1	
			1	
			1	
Total for Week				

EQUIPMENT/PROPERTY EXPENSES				
Date	Name and Description	Check # or Credit Card	Acct #	Amount
			2	
			2	
			2	
			2	
			2	
			2	
			2	
			2	
			2	
			2	
			2	
Total for Week				

PAYROLL EXPENSES				
Date	Employee	Check #	Acct #	Net Pay
			16	
			16	
			16	
			16	
Total for Week				

WEEKLY EXPENSE AND INCOME RECORD

Week Ending On _____ , 20 _____

WEEKLY INCOME OR RETURNS

Date	Name and Description	Check # or Cash	Acct #	Amount	
Total for Week					

EXPENSE TOTALS

#	Account	Prior Week Total	Total for Week	Total to Date
Non-Deductible Expenses				
1	Inventory			
2	Equipment/Property			
3	Loans/Notes Paid			
4	Federal Income Tax			
5	Personal Expense			
6				
	Sub-Total			

#	Account	Prior Week Total	Total for Week	Total to Date
Deductible Expenses				
7	Advertising			
8	Auto/Truck/Travel			
9	Bank Fees			
10	Contributions			
11	Lodging			
12	Insurance			
13	Interest Paid			
14	Legal/Professional			
15	Meals/Entertainment			
16	Payroll (Net Pay)			
17	Payroll (Deductions)			
18	Postage/Freight			
19	Rent			
20	Repairs/Maintenance			
21	Taxes (Sales)			
22	Taxes (Other)			
23	Supplies/Tools			
24	Telephone/Internet			
25	Utilities			
26				
27				
	Sub-Total			

INCOME TOTALS

#	Account	Prior Week Total	Total for Week	Total to Date
1	Sale of Goods Income			
2	Service/Labor Income			
3	Miscellaneous Income			
4	Returns (deduct)	( )	( )	( )

Prior Week Total		
Total for Week		
Total to Date		

Prior Week Total		
Total for Week		
Total to Date		

WEEKLY EXPENSE AND INCOME RECORD

Week Ending On _____ , 20 _____

GENERAL EXPENSES

Date	Name and Description	Check # or Credit Card	Acct #	Amount
Total for Week				

INVENTORY EXPENSES

Date	Name and Description	Check # or Credit Card	Acct #	Amount
			1	
			1	
			1	
			1	
			1	
			1	
			1	
			1	
			1	
			1	
			1	
			1	
Total for Week				

EQUIPMENT/PROPERTY EXPENSES

Date	Name and Description	Check # or Credit Card	Acct #	Amount
			2	
			2	
			2	
			2	
			2	
			2	
			2	
			2	
			2	
			2	
			2	
Total for Week				

PAYROLL EXPENSES

Date	Employee	Check #	Acct #	Net Pay
			16	
			16	
			16	
			16	
Total for Week				

WEEKLY EXPENSE AND INCOME RECORD

Week Ending On _____ , 20 ____

WEEKLY INCOME OR RETURNS

Date	Name and Description	Check # or Cash	Acct #	Amount
	Total for Week			

INCOME TOTALS

#	Account	Prior Week Total	Total for Week	Total to Date
1	Sale of Goods Income			
2	Service/Labor Income			
3	Miscellaneous Income			
4	Returns (deduct)	( )	( )	( )
	Prior Week Total			
	Total for Week			
	Total to Date			

EXPENSE TOTALS

#	Account	Prior Week Total	Total for Week	Total to Date
	Non-Deductible Expenses			
1	Inventory			
2	Equipment/Property			
3	Loans/Notes Paid			
4	Federal Income Tax			
5	Personal Expense			
6				
	Sub-Total			

#	Account	Prior Week Total	Total for Week	Total to Date
	Deductible Expenses			
7	Advertising			
8	Auto/Truck/Travel			
9	Bank Fees			
10	Contributions			
11	Lodging			
12	Insurance			
13	Interest Paid			
14	Legal/Professional			
15	Meals/Entertainment			
16	Payroll (Net Pay)			
17	Payroll (Deductions)			
18	Postage/Freight			
19	Rent			
20	Repairs/Maintenance			
21	Taxes (Sales)			
22	Taxes (Other)			
23	Supplies/Tools			
24	Telephone/Internet			
25	Utilities			
26				
27				
	Sub-Total			
	Prior Week Total			
	Total for Week			
	Total to Date			

WEEKLY EXPENSE AND INCOME RECORD

Week Ending On _____ , 20 _____

GENERAL EXPENSES

Date	Name and Description	Check # or Credit Card	Acct #	Amount	
Total for Week					

INVENTORY EXPENSES

Date	Name and Description	Check # or Credit Card	Acct #	Amount	
			1		
			1		
			1		
			1		
			1		
			1		
			1		
			1		
			1		
			1		
			1		
			1		
Total for Week					

EQUIPMENT/PROPERTY EXPENSES

Date	Name and Description	Check # or Credit Card	Acct #	Amount	
			2		
			2		
			2		
			2		
			2		
			2		
			2		
			2		
			2		
			2		
			2		
Total for Week					

PAYROLL EXPENSES

Date	Employee	Check #	Acct #	Net Pay	
			16		
			16		
			16		
			16		
Total for Week					

WEEKLY EXPENSE AND INCOME RECORD

Week Ending On _____ , 20 _____

WEEKLY INCOME OR RETURNS

Date	Name and Description	Check # or Cash	Acct #	Amount
Total for Week				

INCOME TOTALS

#	Account	Prior Week Total	Total for Week	Total to Date
1	Sale of Goods Income			
2	Service/Labor Income			
3	Miscellaneous Income			
4	Returns (deduct)	( )	( )	( )

Prior Week Total	
Total for Week	
Total to Date	

EXPENSE TOTALS

#	Account	Prior Week Total	Total for Week	Total to Date
Non Deductible Expenses				
1	Inventory			
2	Equipment/Property			
3	Loans/Notes Paid			
4	Federal Income Tax			
5	Personal Expense			
6				
	Sub-Total			

#	Account	Prior Week Total	Total for Week	Total to Date
Deductible Expenses				
7	Advertising			
8	Auto/Truck/Travel			
9	Bank Fees			
10	Contributions			
11	Lodging			
12	Insurance			
13	Interest Paid			
14	Legal/Professional			
15	Meals/Entertainment			
16	Payroll (Net Pay)			
17	Payroll (Deductions)			
18	Postage/Freight			
19	Rent			
20	Repairs/Maintenance			
21	Taxes (Sales)			
22	Taxes (Other)			
23	Supplies/Tools			
24	Telephone/Internet			
25	Utilities			
26				
27				
	Sub-Total			

Prior Week Total	
Total for Week	
Total to Date	

WEEKLY EXPENSE AND INCOME RECORD

Week Ending On _____ , 20 _____

GENERAL EXPENSES

Date	Name and Description	Check # or Credit Card	Acct #	Amount
Total for Week				

INVENTORY EXPENSES

Date	Name and Description	Check # or Credit Card	Acct #	Amount
			1	
			1	
			1	
			1	
			1	
			1	
			1	
			1	
			1	
			1	
			1	
			1	
Total for Week				

EQUIPMENT/PROPERTY EXPENSES

Date	Name and Description	Check # or Credit Card	Acct #	Amount
			2	
			2	
			2	
			2	
			2	
			2	
			2	
			2	
			2	
			2	
Total for Week				

PAYROLL EXPENSES

Date	Employee	Check #	Acct #	Net Pay
			16	
			16	
			16	
			16	
Total for Week				

WEEKLY EXPENSE AND INCOME RECORD

Week Ending On _____ , 20 _____

WEEKLY INCOME OR RETURNS

Date	Name and Description	Check # or Cash	Acct #	Amount	
		Total for Week			

INCOME TOTALS

#	Account	Prior Week Total	Total for Week	Total to Date
1	Sale of Goods Income			
2	Service/Labor Income			
3	Miscellaneous Income			
4	Returns (deduct)	( )	( )	( )

Prior Week Total	
Total for Week	
Total to Date	

EXPENSE TOTALS

#	Account	Prior Week Total	Total for Week	Total to Date
Non Deductible Expenses				
1	Inventory			
2	Equipment/Property			
3	Loans/Notes Paid			
4	Federal Income Tax			
5	Personal Expense			
6				
	Sub-Total			

#	Account	Prior Week Total	Total for Week	Total to Date
Deductible Expenses				
7	Advertising			
8	Auto/Truck/Travel			
9	Bank Fees			
10	Contributions			
11	Lodging			
12	Insurance			
13	Interest Paid			
14	Legal/Professional			
15	Meals/Entertainment			
16	Payroll (Net Pay)			
17	Payroll (Deductions)			
18	Postage/Freight			
19	Rent			
20	Repairs/Maintenance			
21	Taxes (Sales)			
22	Taxes (Other)			
23	Supplies/Tools			
24	Telephone/Internet			
25	Utilities			
26				
27				
	Sub-Total			

Prior Week Total	
Total for Week	
Total to Date	

WEEKLY EXPENSE AND INCOME RECORD

Week Ending On _____ , 20 _____

GENERAL EXPENSES

Date	Name and Description	Check # or Credit Card	Acct #	Amount	
	Total for Week				

INVENTORY EXPENSES

Date	Name and Description	Check # or Credit Card	Acct #	Amount	
			1		
			1		
			1		
			1		
			1		
			1		
			1		
			1		
			1		
			1		
			1		
			1		
	Total for Week				

EQUIPMENT/PROPERTY EXPENSES

Date	Name and Description	Check # or Credit Card	Acct #	Amount	
			2		
			2		
			2		
			2		
			2		
			2		
			2		
			2		
			2		
			2		
	Total for Week				

PAYROLL EXPENSES

Date	Employee	Check #	Acct #	Net Pay	
			16		
			16		
			16		
			16		
	Total for Week				

WEEKLY EXPENSE AND INCOME RECORD

Week Ending On _____ , 20 _____

WEEKLY INCOME OR RETURNS

Date	Name and Description	Check # or Cash	Acct #	Amount
		Total for Week		

INCOME TOTALS

#	Account	Prior Week Total	Total for Week	Total to Date
1	Sale of Goods Income			
2	Service/Labor Income			
3	Miscellaneous Income			
4	Returns (deduct)	( )	( )	( )

Prior Week Total	
Total for Week	
Total to Date	

EXPENSE TOTALS

#	Account	Prior Week Total	Total for Week	Total to Date
Non-Deductible Expenses				
1	Inventory			
2	Equipment/Property			
3	Loans/Notes Paid			
4	Federal Income Tax			
5	Personal Expense			
6				
	Sub-Total			

#	Account	Prior Week Total	Total for Week	Total to Date
Deductible Expenses				
7	Advertising			
8	Auto/Truck/Travel			
9	Bank Fees			
10	Contributions			
11	Lodging			
12	Insurance			
13	Interest Paid			
14	Legal/Professional			
15	Meals/Entertainment			
16	Payroll (Net Pay)			
17	Payroll (Deductions)			
18	Postage/Freight			
19	Rent			
20	Repairs/Maintenance			
21	Taxes (Sales)			
22	Taxes (Other)			
23	Supplies/Tools			
24	Telephone/Internet			
25	Utilities			
26				
27				
	Sub-Total			

Prior Week Total	
Total for Week	
Total to Date	

WEEKLY EXPENSE AND INCOME RECORD

Week Ending On _____ , 20 _____

GENERAL EXPENSES

Date	Name and Description	Check # or Credit Card	Acct #	Amount	
Total for Week					

INVENTORY EXPENSES

Date	Name and Description	Check # or Credit Card	Acct #	Amount	
			1		
			1		
			1		
			1		
			1		
			1		
			1		
			1		
			1		
			1		
			1		
			1		
Total for Week					

EQUIPMENT/PROPERTY EXPENSES

Date	Name and Description	Check # or Credit Card	Acct #	Amount	
			2		
			2		
			2		
			2		
			2		
			2		
			2		
			2		
			2		
			2		
			2		
Total for Week					

PAYROLL EXPENSES

Date	Employee	Check #	Acct #	Net Pay	
			16		
			16		
			16		
			16		
Total for Week					

WEEKLY EXPENSE AND INCOME RECORD

Week Ending On _____ , 20 _____

WEEKLY INCOME OR RETURNS

Date	Name and Description	Check # or Cash	Acct #	Amount
Total for Week				

EXPENSE TOTALS

#	Account	Prior Week Total	Total for Week	Total to Date
Non Deductible Expenses				
1	Inventory			
2	Equipment/Property			
3	Loans/Notes Paid			
4	Federal Income Tax			
5	Personal Expense			
6				
	Sub-Total			

#	Account	Prior Week Total	Total for Week	Total to Date
Deductible Expenses				
7	Advertising			
8	Auto/Truck/Travel			
9	Bank Fees			
10	Contributions			
11	Lodging			
12	Insurance			
13	Interest Paid			
14	Legal/Professional			
15	Meals/Entertainment			
16	Payroll (Net Pay)			
17	Payroll (Deductions)			
18	Postage/Freight			
19	Rent			
20	Repairs/Maintenance			
21	Taxes (Sales)			
22	Taxes (Other)			
23	Supplies/Tools			
24	Telephone/Internet			
25	Utilities			
26				
27				
	Sub-Total			

INCOME TOTALS

#	Account	Prior Week Total	Total for Week	Total to Date
1	Sale of Goods Income			
2	Service/Labor Income			
3	Miscellaneous Income			
4	Returns (deduct)	( )	( )	( )

Prior Week Total		
Total for Week		
Total to Date		

Prior Week Total		
Total for Week		
Total to Date		

WEEKLY EXPENSE AND INCOME RECORD

Week Ending On _____ , 20 _____

GENERAL EXPENSES

Date	Name and Description	Check # or Credit Card	Acct #	Amount	
Total for Week					

INVENTORY EXPENSES

Date	Name and Description	Check # or Credit Card	Acct #	Amount	
			1		
			1		
			1		
			1		
			1		
			1		
			1		
			1		
			1		
			1		
			1		
			1		
Total for Week					

EQUIPMENT/PROPERTY EXPENSES

Date	Name and Description	Check # or Credit Card	Acct #	Amount	
			2		
			2		
			2		
			2		
			2		
			2		
			2		
			2		
			2		
			2		
			2		
Total for Week					

PAYROLL EXPENSES

Date	Employee	Check #	Acct #	Net Pay	
			16		
			16		
			16		
			16		
Total for Week					

WEEKLY EXPENSE AND INCOME RECORD

Week Ending On _____ , 20 _____

WEEKLY INCOME OR RETURNS

Date	Name and Description	Check # or Cash	Acct #	Amount
	Total for Week			

EXPENSE TOTALS

#	Account	Prior Week Total	Total for Week	Total to Date
Non-Deductible Expenses				
1	Inventory			
2	Equipment/Property			
3	Loans/Notes Paid			
4	Federal Income Tax			
5	Personal Expense			
6				
	Sub-Total			

#	Account	Prior Week Total	Total for Week	Total to Date
Deductible Expenses				
7	Advertising			
8	Auto/Truck/Travel			
9	Bank Fees			
10	Contributions			
11	Lodging			
12	Insurance			
13	Interest Paid			
14	Legal/Professional			
15	Meals/Entertainment			
16	Payroll (Net Pay)			
17	Payroll (Deductions)			
18	Postage/Freight			
19	Rent			
20	Repairs/Maintenance			
21	Taxes (Sales)			
22	Taxes (Other)			
23	Supplies/Tools			
24	Telephone/Internet			
25	Utilities			
26				
27				
	Sub-Total			

INCOME TOTALS

#	Account	Prior Week Total	Total for Week	Total to Date
1	Sale of Goods Income			
2	Service/Labor Income			
3	Miscellaneous Income			
4	Returns (deduct)	( )	( )	( )

Prior Week Total	
Total for Week	
Total to Date	

Prior Week Total	
Total for Week	
Total to Date	

WEEKLY EXPENSE AND INCOME RECORD

Week Ending On _____ , 20 _____

GENERAL EXPENSES

Date	Name and Description	Check # or Credit Card	Acct #	Amount	
Total for Week					

INVENTORY EXPENSES

Date	Name and Description	Check # or Credit Card	Acct #	Amount	
			1		
			1		
			1		
			1		
			1		
			1		
			1		
			1		
			1		
			1		
			1		
			1		
Total for Week					

EQUIPMENT/PROPERTY EXPENSES

Date	Name and Description	Check # or Credit Card	Acct #	Amount	
			2		
			2		
			2		
			2		
			2		
			2		
			2		
			2		
			2		
			2		
Total for Week					

PAYROLL EXPENSES

Date	Employee	Check #	Acct #	Net Pay	
			16		
			16		
			16		
			16		
Total for Week					

WEEKLY EXPENSE AND INCOME RECORD

Week Ending On _____ , 20 ____

WEEKLY INCOME OR RETURNS

Date	Name and Description	Check # or Cash	Acct #	Amount	
	Total for Week				

INCOME TOTALS

#	Account	Prior Week Total	Total for Week	Total to Date
1	Sale of Goods Income			
2	Service/Labor Income			
3	Miscellaneous Income			
4	Returns (deduct)	( )	( )	( )
	Prior Week Total			
	Total for Week			
	Total to Date			

EXPENSE TOTALS

#	Account	Prior Week Total	Total for Week	Total to Date
Non-Deductible Expenses				
1	Inventory			
2	Equipment/Property			
3	Loans/Notes Paid			
4	Federal Income Tax			
5	Personal Expense			
6				
	Sub-Total			

#	Account	Prior Week Total	Total for Week	Total to Date
Deductible Expenses				
7	Advertising			
8	Auto/Truck/Travel			
9	Bank Fees			
10	Contributions			
11	Lodging			
12	Insurance			
13	Interest Paid			
14	Legal/Professional			
15	Meals/Entertainment			
16	Payroll (Net Pay)			
17	Payroll (Deductions)			
18	Postage/Freight			
19	Rent			
20	Repairs/Maintenance			
21	Taxes (Sales)			
22	Taxes (Other)			
23	Supplies/Tools			
24	Telephone/Internet			
25	Utilities			
26				
27				
	Sub-Total			
	Prior Week Total			
	Total for Week			
	Total to Date			

WEEKLY EXPENSE AND INCOME RECORD

Week Ending On _____ , 20 _____

GENERAL EXPENSES

Date	Name and Description	Check # or Credit Card	Acct #	Amount	
Total for Week					

INVENTORY EXPENSES

Date	Name and Description	Check # or Credit Card	Acct #	Amount	
			1		
			1		
			1		
			1		
			1		
			1		
			1		
			1		
			1		
			1		
			1		
			1		
Total for Week					

EQUIPMENT/PROPERTY EXPENSES

Date	Name and Description	Check # or Credit Card	Acct #	Amount	
			2		
			2		
			2		
			2		
			2		
			2		
			2		
			2		
			2		
			2		
			2		
Total for Week					

PAYROLL EXPENSES

Date	Employee	Check #	Acct #	Net Pay	
			16		
			16		
			16		
			16		
Total for Week					

WEEKLY EXPENSE AND INCOME RECORD

Week Ending On _____ , 20 ____

WEEKLY INCOME OR RETURNS

Date	Name and Description	Check # or Cash	Acct #	Amount	
Total for Week					

INCOME TOTALS

#	Account	Prior Week Total		Total for Week		Total to Date	
1	Sale of Goods Income						
2	Service/Labor Income						
3	Miscellaneous Income						
4	Returns (deduct)	(	)	(	)	(	)

Prior Week Total		
Total for Week		
Total to Date		

EXPENSE TOTALS

#	Account	Prior Week Total		Total for Week		Total to Date	
Non-Deductible Expenses							
1	Inventory						
2	Equipment/Property						
3	Loans/Notes Paid						
4	Federal Income Tax						
5	Personal Expense						
6							
	Sub-Total						

#	Account	Prior Week Total		Total for Week		Total to Date	
Deductible Expenses							
7	Advertising						
8	Auto/Truck/Travel						
9	Bank Fees						
10	Contributions						
11	Lodging						
12	Insurance						
13	Interest Paid						
14	Legal/Professional						
15	Meals/Entertainment						
16	Payroll (Net Pay)						
17	Payroll (Deductions)						
18	Postage/Freight						
19	Rent						
20	Repairs/Maintenance						
21	Taxes (Sales)						
22	Taxes (Other)						
23	Supplies/Tools						
24	Telephone/Internet						
25	Utilities						
26							
27							
	Sub-Total						

Prior Week Total		
Total for Week		
Total to Date		

WEEKLY EXPENSE AND INCOME RECORD

Week Ending On _____ , 20 _____

GENERAL EXPENSES

Date	Name and Description	Check # or Credit Card	Acct #	Amount	
	Total for Week				

INVENTORY EXPENSES

Date	Name and Description	Check # or Credit Card	Acct #	Amount	
			1		
			1		
			1		
			1		
			1		
			1		
			1		
			1		
			1		
			1		
			1		
			1		
	Total for Week				

EQUIPMENT/PROPERTY EXPENSES

Date	Name and Description	Check # or Credit Card	Acct #	Amount	
			2		
			2		
			2		
			2		
			2		
			2		
			2		
			2		
			2		
			2		
	Total for Week				

PAYROLL EXPENSES

Date	Employee	Check #	Acct #	Net Pay	
			16		
			16		
			16		
			16		
	Total for Week				

WEEKLY EXPENSE AND INCOME RECORD

Week Ending On _____ , 20 ____

WEEKLY INCOME OR RETURNS

Date	Name and Description	Check # or Cash	Acct #	Amount	
Total for Week					

INCOME TOTALS

#	Account	Prior Week Total	Total for Week	Total to Date
1	Sale of Goods Income			
2	Service/Labor Income			
3	Miscellaneous Income			
4	Returns (deduct)	( )	( )	( )

Prior Week Total	
Total for Week	
Total to Date	

EXPENSE TOTALS

#	Account	Prior Week Total	Total for Week	Total to Date
	Non-Deductible Expenses			
1	Inventory			
2	Equipment/Property			
3	Loans/Notes Paid			
4	Federal Income Tax			
5	Personal Expense			
6				
	Sub-Total			

#	Account	Prior Week Total	Total for Week	Total to Date
	Deductible Expenses			
7	Advertising			
8	Auto/Truck/Travel			
9	Bank Fees			
10	Contributions			
11	Lodging			
12	Insurance			
13	Interest Paid			
14	Legal/Professional			
15	Meals/Entertainment			
16	Payroll (Net Pay)			
17	Payroll (Deductions)			
18	Postage/Freight			
19	Rent			
20	Repairs/Maintenance			
21	Taxes (Sales)			
22	Taxes (Other)			
23	Supplies/Tools			
24	Telephone/Internet			
25	Utilities			
26				
27				
	Sub-Total			

Prior Week Total	
Total for Week	
Total to Date	

WEEKLY EXPENSE AND INCOME RECORD

Week Ending On _____ , 20 _____

GENERAL EXPENSES

Date	Name and Description	Check # or Credit Card	Acct #		Amount	
Total for Week						

INVENTORY EXPENSES

Date	Name and Description	Check # or Credit Card	Acct #		Amount	
			1			
			1			
			1			
			1			
			1			
			1			
			1			
			1			
			1			
			1			
			1			
			1			
Total for Week						

EQUIPMENT/PROPERTY EXPENSES

Date	Name and Description	Check # or Credit Card	Acct #		Amount	
			2			
			2			
			2			
			2			
			2			
			2			
			2			
			2			
			2			
			2			
			2			
Total for Week						

PAYROLL EXPENSES

Date	Employee	Check #	Acct #	Net Pay	
			16		
			16		
			16		
			16		
Total for Week					

WEEKLY EXPENSE AND INCOME RECORD

Week Ending On _____ , 20 _____

WEEKLY INCOME OR RETURNS

Date	Name and Description	Check # or Cash	Acct #	Amount	
Total for Week					

INCOME TOTALS

#	Account	Prior Week Total	Total for Week	Total to Date
1	Sale of Goods Income			
2	Service/Labor Income			
3	Miscellaneous Income			
4	Returns (deduct)	( )	( )	( )

	Prior Week Total	
	Total for Week	
	Total to Date	

EXPENSE TOTALS

#	Account	Prior Week Total	Total for Week	Total to Date
Non-Deductible Expenses				
1	Inventory			
2	Equipment/Property			
3	Loans/Notes Paid			
4	Federal Income Tax			
5	Personal Expense			
6				
	Sub-Total			

#	Account	Prior Week Total	Total for Week	Total to Date
Deductible Expenses				
7	Advertising			
8	Auto/Truck/Travel			
9	Bank Fees			
10	Contributions			
11	Lodging			
12	Insurance			
13	Interest Paid			
14	Legal/Professional			
15	Meals/Entertainment			
16	Payroll (Net Pay)			
17	Payroll (Deductions)			
18	Postage/Freight			
19	Rent			
20	Repairs/Maintenance			
21	Taxes (Sales)			
22	Taxes (Other)			
23	Supplies/Tools			
24	Telephone/Internet			
25	Utilities			
26				
27				
	Sub-Total			

	Prior Week Total	
	Total for Week	
	Total to Date	

WEEKLY EXPENSE AND INCOME RECORD

Week Ending On _____ , 20 _____

GENERAL EXPENSES

Date	Name and Description	Check # or Credit Card	Acct #	Amount	
Total for Week					

INVENTORY EXPENSES

Date	Name and Description	Check # or Credit Card	Acct #	Amount	
			1		
			1		
			1		
			1		
			1		
			1		
			1		
			1		
			1		
			1		
			1		
			1		
Total for Week					

EQUIPMENT/PROPERTY EXPENSES

Date	Name and Description	Check # or Credit Card	Acct #	Amount	
			2		
			2		
			2		
			2		
			2		
			2		
			2		
			2		
			2		
			2		
			2		
Total for Week					

PAYROLL EXPENSES

Date	Employee	Check #	Acct #	Net Pay	
			16		
			16		
			16		
			16		
Total for Week					

WEEKLY EXPENSE AND INCOME RECORD

Week Ending On _____ , 20 ____

WEEKLY INCOME OR RETURNS

Date	Name and Description	Check # or Cash	Acct #	Amount	
Total for Week					

INCOME TOTALS

#	Account	Prior Week Total	Total for Week	Total to Date	
1	Sale of Goods Income				
2	Service/Labor Income				
3	Miscellaneous Income				
4	Returns (deduct)	( )	( )	( )	
	Prior Week Total				
	Total for Week				
	Total to Date				

EXPENSE TOTALS

#	Account	Prior Week Total	Total for Week	Total to Date	
	Non-Deductible Expenses				
1	Inventory				
2	Equipment/Property				
3	Loans/Notes Paid				
4	Federal Income Tax				
5	Personal Expense				
6					
	Sub-Total				

#	Account	Prior Week Total	Total for Week	Total to Date	
	Deductible Expenses				
7	Advertising				
8	Auto/Truck/Travel				
9	Bank Fees				
10	Contributions				
11	Lodging				
12	Insurance				
13	Interest Paid				
14	Legal/Professional				
15	Meals/Entertainment				
16	Payroll (Net Pay)				
17	Payroll (Deductions)				
18	Postage/Freight				
19	Rent				
20	Repairs/Maintenance				
21	Taxes (Sales)				
22	Taxes (Other)				
23	Supplies/Tools				
24	Telephone/Internet				
25	Utilities				
26					
27					
	Sub-Total				
	Prior Week Total				
	Total for Week				
	Total to Date				

WEEKLY EXPENSE AND INCOME RECORD

Week Ending On _____ , 20 ____

GENERAL EXPENSES

Date	Name and Description	Check # or Credit Card	Acct #	Amount	
	Total for Week				

INVENTORY EXPENSES

Date	Name and Description	Check # or Credit Card	Acct #	Amount	
			1		
			1		
			1		
			1		
			1		
			1		
			1		
			1		
			1		
			1		
			1		
			1		
	Total for Week				

EQUIPMENT/PROPERTY EXPENSES

Date	Name and Description	Check # or Credit Card	Acct #	Amount	
			2		
			2		
			2		
			2		
			2		
			2		
			2		
			2		
			2		
			2		
	Total for Week				

PAYROLL EXPENSES

Date	Employee	Check #	Acct #	Net Pay	
			16		
			16		
			16		
			16		
	Total for Week				

WEEKLY EXPENSE AND INCOME RECORD

Week Ending On _____ , 20 ____

WEEKLY INCOME OR RETURNS

Date	Name and Description	Check # or Cash	Acct #	Amount
	Total for Week			

EXPENSE TOTALS

#	Account	Prior Week Total	Total for Week	Total to Date
Non-Deductible Expenses				
1	Inventory			
2	Equipment/Property			
3	Loans/Notes Paid			
4	Federal Income Tax			
5	Personal Expense			
6				
	Sub-Total			

#	Account	Prior Week Total	Total for Week	Total to Date
Deductible Expenses				
7	Advertising			
8	Auto/Truck/Travel			
9	Bank Fees			
10	Contributions			
11	Lodging			
12	Insurance			
13	Interest Paid			
14	Legal/Professional			
15	Meals/Entertainment			
16	Payroll (Net Pay)			
17	Payroll (Deductions)			
18	Postage/Freight			
19	Rent			
20	Repairs/Maintenance			
21	Taxes (Sales)			
22	Taxes (Other)			
23	Supplies/Tools			
24	Telephone/Internet			
25	Utilities			
26				
27				
	Sub-Total			

INCOME TOTALS

#	Account	Prior Week Total	Total for Week	Total to Date
1	Sale of Goods Income			
2	Service/Labor Income			
3	Miscellaneous Income			
4	Returns (deduct)	( )	( )	( )

Prior Week Total		
Total for Week		
Total to Date		

Prior Week Total		
Total for Week		
Total to Date		

WEEKLY EXPENSE AND INCOME RECORD

Week Ending On _____ , 20 _____

GENERAL EXPENSES

Date	Name and Description	Check # or Credit Card	Acct #	Amount	
Total for Week					

INVENTORY EXPENSES

Date	Name and Description	Check # or Credit Card	Acct #	Amount	
			1		
			1		
			1		
			1		
			1		
			1		
			1		
			1		
			1		
			1		
			1		
			1		
Total for Week					

EQUIPMENT/PROPERTY EXPENSES

Date	Name and Description	Check # or Credit Card	Acct #	Amount	
			2		
			2		
			2		
			2		
			2		
			2		
			2		
			2		
			2		
			2		
			2		
Total for Week					

PAYROLL EXPENSES

Date	Employee	Check #	Acct #	Net Pay	
			16		
			16		
			16		
			16		
Total for Week					

WEEKLY EXPENSE AND INCOME RECORD

Week Ending On _____ , 20 _____

WEEKLY INCOME OR RETURNS

Date	Name and Description	Check # or Cash	Acct #	Amount	
	Total for Week				

INCOME TOTALS

#	Account	Prior Week Total	Total for Week	Total to Date	
1	Sale of Goods Income				
2	Service/Labor Income				
3	Miscellaneous Income				
4	Returns (deduct)	( )	( )	( )	

Prior Week Total			
Total for Week			
Total to Date			

EXPENSE TOTALS

#	Account	Prior Week Total	Total for Week	Total to Date	
Non-Deductible Expenses					
1	Inventory				
2	Equipment/Property				
3	Loans/Notes Paid				
4	Federal Income Tax				
5	Personal Expense				
6					
	Sub-Total				

#	Account	Prior Week Total	Total for Week	Total to Date	
Deductible Expenses					
7	Advertising				
8	Auto/Truck/Travel				
9	Bank Fees				
10	Contributions				
11	Lodging				
12	Insurance				
13	Interest Paid				
14	Legal/Professional				
15	Meals/Entertainment				
16	Payroll (Net Pay)				
17	Payroll (Deductions)				
18	Postage/Freight				
19	Rent				
20	Repairs/Maintenance				
21	Taxes (Sales)				
22	Taxes (Other)				
23	Supplies/Tools				
24	Telephone/Internet				
25	Utilities				
26					
27					
	Sub-Total				

Prior Week Total			
Total for Week			
Total to Date			

WEEKLY EXPENSE AND INCOME RECORD

Week Ending On _____ , 20 _____

GENERAL EXPENSES

Date	Name and Description	Check # or Credit Card	Acct #	Amount	
Total for Week					

INVENTORY EXPENSES

Date	Name and Description	Check # or Credit Card	Acct #	Amount	
			1		
			1		
			1		
			1		
			1		
			1		
			1		
			1		
			1		
			1		
			1		
Total for Week					

EQUIPMENT/PROPERTY EXPENSES

Date	Name and Description	Check # or Credit Card	Acct #	Amount	
			2		
			2		
			2		
			2		
			2		
			2		
			2		
			2		
			2		
			2		
			2		
Total for Week					

PAYROLL EXPENSES

Date	Employee	Check #	Acct #	Net Pay	
			16		
			16		
			16		
			16		
Total for Week					

WEEKLY EXPENSE AND INCOME RECORD

Week Ending On _____ , 20 ____

WEEKLY INCOME OR RETURNS

Date	Name and Description	Check # or Cash	Acct #	Amount	
		Total for Week			

INCOME TOTALS

#	Account	Prior Week Total	Total for Week	Total to Date	
1	Sale of Goods Income				
2	Service/Labor Income				
3	Miscellaneous Income				
4	Returns (deduct)	( )	( )	( )	

Prior Week Total		
Total for Week		
Total to Date		

EXPENSE TOTALS

#	Account	Prior Week Total	Total for Week	Total to Date	
Non-Deductible Expenses					
1	Inventory				
2	Equipment/Property				
3	Loans/Notes Paid				
4	Federal Income Tax				
5	Personal Expense				
6					
	Sub-Total				

#	Account	Prior Week Total	Total for Week	Total to Date	
Deductible Expenses					
7	Advertising				
8	Auto/Truck/Travel				
9	Bank Fees				
10	Contributions				
11	Lodging				
12	Insurance				
13	Interest Paid				
14	Legal/Professional				
15	Meals/Entertainment				
16	Payroll (Net Pay)				
17	Payroll (Deductions)				
18	Postage/Freight				
19	Rent				
20	Repairs/Maintenance				
21	Taxes (Sales)				
22	Taxes (Other)				
23	Supplies/Tools				
24	Telephone/Internet				
25	Utilities				
26					
27					
	Sub-Total				

Prior Week Total		
Total for Week		
Total to Date		

WEEKLY EXPENSE AND INCOME RECORD

Week Ending On _____ , 20 ____

GENERAL EXPENSES

Date	Name and Description	Check # or Credit Card	Acct #	Amount	
Total for Week					

INVENTORY EXPENSES

Date	Name and Description	Check # or Credit Card	Acct #	Amount	
			1		
			1		
			1		
			1		
			1		
			1		
			1		
			1		
			1		
			1		
			1		
Total for Week					

EQUIPMENT/PROPERTY EXPENSES

Date	Name and Description	Check # or Credit Card	Acct #	Amount	
			2		
			2		
			2		
			2		
			2		
			2		
			2		
			2		
			2		
			2		
			2		
Total for Week					

PAYROLL EXPENSES

Date	Employee	Check #	Acct #	Net Pay	
			16		
			16		
			16		
			16		
Total for Week					

WEEKLY EXPENSE AND INCOME RECORD

Week Ending On _____ , 20 ____

WEEKLY INCOME OR RETURNS

Date	Name and Description	Check # or Cash	Acct #	Amount	
	Total for Week				

INCOME TOTALS

#	Account	Prior Week Total	Total for Week	Total to Date
1	Sale of Goods Income			
2	Service/Labor Income			
3	Miscellaneous Income			
4	Returns (deduct)	( )	( )	( )

Prior Week Total		
Total for Week		
Total to Date		

EXPENSE TOTALS

#	Account	Prior Week Total	Total for Week	Total to Date
Non-Deductible Expenses				
1	Inventory			
2	Equipment/Property			
3	Loans/Notes Paid			
4	Federal Income Tax			
5	Personal Expense			
6				
	Sub-Total			

#	Account	Prior Week Total	Total for Week	Total to Date
Deductible Expenses				
7	Advertising			
8	Auto/Truck/Travel			
9	Bank Fees			
10	Contributions			
11	Lodging			
12	Insurance			
13	Interest Paid			
14	Legal/Professional			
15	Meals/Entertainment			
16	Payroll (Net Pay)			
17	Payroll (Deductions)			
18	Postage/Freight			
19	Rent			
20	Repairs/Maintenance			
21	Taxes (Sales)			
22	Taxes (Other)			
23	Supplies/Tools			
24	Telephone/Internet			
25	Utilities			
26				
27				
	Sub-Total			

Prior Week Total		
Total for Week		
Total to Date		

WEEKLY EXPENSE AND INCOME RECORD

Week Ending On _____ , 20 _____

GENERAL EXPENSES

Date	Name and Description	Check # or Credit Card	Acct #	Amount	
	Total for Week				

INVENTORY EXPENSES

Date	Name and Description	Check # or Credit Card	Acct #	Amount	
			1		
			1		
			1		
			1		
			1		
			1		
			1		
			1		
			1		
			1		
			1		
			1		
	Total for Week				

EQUIPMENT/PROPERTY EXPENSES

Date	Name and Description	Check # or Credit Card	Acct #	Amount	
			2		
			2		
			2		
			2		
			2		
			2		
			2		
			2		
			2		
			2		
			2		
	Total for Week				

PAYROLL EXPENSES

Date	Employee	Check #	Acct #	Net Pay	
			16		
			16		
			16		
			16		
	Total for Week				

WEEKLY EXPENSE AND INCOME RECORD

Week Ending On _____ , 20 ____

WEEKLY INCOME OR RETURNS

Date	Name and Description	Check # or Cash	Acct #	Amount	
Total for Week					

INCOME TOTALS

#	Account	Prior Week Total	Total for Week	Total to Date
1	Sale of Goods Income			
2	Service/Labor Income			
3	Miscellaneous Income			
4	Returns (deduct)	( )	( )	( )

Prior Week Total	
Total for Week	
Total to Date	

EXPENSE TOTALS

#	Account	Prior Week Total	Total for Week	Total to Date
Non-Deductible Expenses				
1	Inventory			
2	Equipment/Property			
3	Loans/Notes Paid			
4	Federal Income Tax			
5	Personal Expense			
6				
Sub-Total				

#	Account	Prior Week Total	Total for Week	Total to Date
Deductible Expenses				
7	Advertising			
8	Auto/Truck/Travel			
9	Bank Fees			
10	Contributions			
11	Lodging			
12	Insurance			
13	Interest Paid			
14	Legal/Professional			
15	Meals/Entertainment			
16	Payroll (Net Pay)			
17	Payroll (Deductions)			
18	Postage/Freight			
19	Rent			
20	Repairs/Maintenance			
21	Taxes (Sales)			
22	Taxes (Other)			
23	Supplies/Tools			
24	Telephone/Internet			
25	Utilities			
26				
27				
Sub-Total				

Prior Week Total	
Total for Week	
Total to Date	

WEEKLY EXPENSE AND INCOME RECORD

Week Ending On _____ , 20 _____

GENERAL EXPENSES

Date	Name and Description	Check # or Credit Card	Acct #	Amount	
	Total for Week				

INVENTORY EXPENSES

Date	Name and Description	Check # or Credit Card	Acct #	Amount	
			1		
			1		
			1		
			1		
			1		
			1		
			1		
			1		
			1		
			1		
			1		
			1		
	Total for Week				

EQUIPMENT/PROPERTY EXPENSES

Date	Name and Description	Check # or Credit Card	Acct #	Amount	
			2		
			2		
			2		
			2		
			2		
			2		
			2		
			2		
			2		
			2		
			2		
	Total for Week				

PAYROLL EXPENSES

Date	Employee	Check #	Acct #	Net Pay	
			16		
			16		
			16		
			16		
	Total for Week				

WEEKLY EXPENSE AND INCOME RECORD

Week Ending On _____ , 20 ____

WEEKLY INCOME OR RETURNS

Date	Name and Description	Check # or Cash	Acct #	Amount	
Total for Week					

INCOME TOTALS

#	Account	Prior Week Total	Total for Week	Total to Date
1	Sale of Goods Income			
2	Service/Labor Income			
3	Miscellaneous Income			
4	Returns (deduct)	( )	( )	( )

Prior Week Total		
Total for Week		
Total to Date		

EXPENSE TOTALS

#	Account	Prior Week Total	Total for Week	Total to Date
Non-Deductible Expenses				
1	Inventory			
2	Equipment/Property			
3	Loans/Notes Paid			
4	Federal Income Tax			
5	Personal Expense			
6				
	Sub-Total			

#	Account	Prior Week Total	Total for Week	Total to Date
Deductible Expenses				
7	Advertising			
8	Auto/Truck/Travel			
9	Bank Fees			
10	Contributions			
11	Lodging			
12	Insurance			
13	Interest Paid			
14	Legal/Professional			
15	Meals/Entertainment			
16	Payroll (Net Pay)			
17	Payroll (Deductions)			
18	Postage/Freight			
19	Rent			
20	Repairs/Maintenance			
21	Taxes (Sales)			
22	Taxes (Other)			
23	Supplies/Tools			
24	Telephone/Internet			
25	Utilities			
26				
27				
	Sub-Total			

Prior Week Total		
Total for Week		
Total to Date		

WEEKLY EXPENSE AND INCOME RECORD

Week Ending On _____ , 20 _____

GENERAL EXPENSES

Date	Name and Description	Check # or Credit Card	Acct #	Amount	
	Total for Week				

INVENTORY EXPENSES

Date	Name and Description	Check # or Credit Card	Acct #	Amount	
			1		
			1		
			1		
			1		
			1		
			1		
			1		
			1		
			1		
			1		
			1		
			1		
	Total for Week				

EQUIPMENT/PROPERTY EXPENSES

Date	Name and Description	Check # or Credit Card	Acct #	Amount	
			2		
			2		
			2		
			2		
			2		
			2		
			2		
			2		
			2		
			2		
	Total for Week				

PAYROLL EXPENSES

Date	Employee	Check #	Acct #	Net Pay	
			16		
			16		
			16		
			16		
	Total for Week				

WEEKLY EXPENSE AND INCOME RECORD

Week Ending On _____ , 20 ___

WEEKLY INCOME OR RETURNS

Date	Name and Description	Check # or Cash	Acct #	Amount	
Total for Week					

EXPENSE TOTALS

#	Account	Prior Week Total	Total for Week	Total to Date	
Non-Deductible Expenses					
1	Inventory				
2	Equipment/Property				
3	Loans/Notes Paid				
4	Federal Income Tax				
5	Personal Expense				
6					
	Sub-Total				

#	Account	Prior Week Total	Total for Week	Total to Date	
Deductible Expenses					
7	Advertising				
8	Auto/Truck/Travel				
9	Bank Fees				
10	Contributions				
11	Lodging				
12	Insurance				
13	Interest Paid				
14	Legal/Professional				
15	Meals/Entertainment				
16	Payroll (Net Pay)				
17	Payroll (Deductions)				
18	Postage/Freight				
19	Rent				
20	Repairs/Maintenance				
21	Taxes (Sales)				
22	Taxes (Other)				
23	Supplies/Tools				
24	Telephone/Internet				
25	Utilities				
26					
27					
	Sub-Total				

INCOME TOTALS

#	Account	Prior Week Total	Total for Week	Total to Date	
1	Sale of Goods Income				
2	Service/Labor Income				
3	Miscellaneous Income				
4	Returns (deduct)	( )	( )	( )	

Prior Week Total		
Total for Week		
Total to Date		

Prior Week Total		
Total for Week		
Total to Date		

WEEKLY EXPENSE AND INCOME RECORD

Week Ending On _____ , 20 ____

GENERAL EXPENSES

Date	Name and Description	Check # or Credit Card	Acct #	Amount	
Total for Week					

INVENTORY EXPENSES

Date	Name and Description	Check # or Credit Card	Acct #	Amount	
			1		
			1		
			1		
			1		
			1		
			1		
			1		
			1		
			1		
			1		
			1		
			1		
Total for Week					

EQUIPMENT/PROPERTY EXPENSES

Date	Name and Description	Check # or Credit Card	Acct #	Amount	
			2		
			2		
			2		
			2		
			2		
			2		
			2		
			2		
			2		
			2		
			2		
Total for Week					

PAYROLL EXPENSES

Date	Employee	Check #	Acct #	Net Pay	
			16		
			16		
			16		
			16		
Total for Week					

WEEKLY EXPENSE AND INCOME RECORD

Week Ending On _____ , 20 _____

WEEKLY INCOME OR RETURNS

Date	Name and Description	Check # or Cash	Acct #	Amount	
		Total for Week			

EXPENSE TOTALS

#	Account	Prior Week Total	Total for Week	Total to Date	
Non-Deductible Expenses					
1	Inventory				
2	Equipment/Property				
3	Loans/Notes Paid				
4	Federal Income Tax				
5	Personal Expense				
6					
	Sub-Total				

#	Account	Prior Week Total	Total for Week	Total to Date	
Deductible Expenses					
7	Advertising				
8	Auto/Truck/Travel				
9	Bank Fees				
10	Contributions				
11	Lodging				
12	Insurance				
13	Interest Paid				
14	Legal/Professional				
15	Meals/Entertainment				
16	Payroll (Net Pay)				
17	Payroll (Deductions)				
18	Postage/Freight				
19	Rent				
20	Repairs/Maintenance				
21	Taxes (Sales)				
22	Taxes (Other)				
23	Supplies/Tools				
24	Telephone/Internet				
25	Utilities				
26					
27					
	Sub-Total				

INCOME TOTALS

#	Account	Prior Week Total	Total for Week	Total to Date	
1	Sale of Goods Income				
2	Service/Labor Income				
3	Miscellaneous Income				
4	Returns (deduct)	( )	( )	( )	

Prior Week Total		
Total for Week		
Total to Date		

Prior Week Total		
Total for Week		
Total to Date		

WEEKLY EXPENSE AND INCOME RECORD

Week Ending On _____ , 20 _____

GENERAL EXPENSES

Date	Name and Description	Check # or Credit Card	Acct #	Amount	
	Total for Week				

INVENTORY EXPENSES

Date	Name and Description	Check # or Credit Card	Acct #	Amount	
			1		
			1		
			1		
			1		
			1		
			1		
			1		
			1		
			1		
			1		
			1		
			1		
Total for Week					

EQUIPMENT/PROPERTY EXPENSES

Date	Name and Description	Check # or Credit Card	Acct #	Amount	
			2		
			2		
			2		
			2		
			2		
			2		
			2		
			2		
			2		
			2		
			2		
Total for Week					

PAYROLL EXPENSES

Date	Employee	Check #	Acct #	Net Pay	
			16		
			16		
			16		
			16		
Total for Week					

WEEKLY EXPENSE AND INCOME RECORD

Week Ending On _____ , 20 _____

WEEKLY INCOME OR RETURNS

Date	Name and Description	Check # or Cash	Acct #	Amount	
		Total for Week			

INCOME TOTALS

#	Account	Prior Week Total	Total for Week	Total to Date	
1	Sale of Goods Income				
2	Service/Labor Income				
3	Miscellaneous Income				
4	Returns (deduct)	( )	( )	( )	

Prior Week Total		
Total for Week		
Total to Date		

EXPENSE TOTALS

#	Account	Prior Week Total	Total for Week	Total to Date	
	Non-Deductible Expenses				
1	Inventory				
2	Equipment/Property				
3	Loans/Notes Paid				
4	Federal Income Tax				
5	Personal Expense				
6					
	Sub-Total				

#	Account	Prior Week Total	Total for Week	Total to Date	
	Deductible Expenses				
7	Advertising				
8	Auto/Truck/Travel				
9	Bank Fees				
10	Contributions				
11	Lodging				
12	Insurance				
13	Interest Paid				
14	Legal/Professional				
15	Meals/Entertainment				
16	Payroll (Net Pay)				
17	Payroll (Deductions)				
18	Postage/Freight				
19	Rent				
20	Repairs/Maintenance				
21	Taxes (Sales)				
22	Taxes (Other)				
23	Supplies/Tools				
24	Telephone/Internet				
25	Utilities				
26					
27					
	Sub-Total				

Prior Week Total		
Total for Week		
Total to Date		

WEEKLY EXPENSE AND INCOME RECORD

Week Ending On _____ , 20 _____

GENERAL EXPENSES

Date	Name and Description	Check # or Credit Card	Acct #	Amount	
Total for Week					

INVENTORY EXPENSES

Date	Name and Description	Check # or Credit Card	Acct #	Amount	
			1		
			1		
			1		
			1		
			1		
			1		
			1		
			1		
			1		
			1		
			1		
			1		
Total for Week					

EQUIPMENT/PROPERTY EXPENSES

Date	Name and Description	Check # or Credit Card	Acct #	Amount	
			2		
			2		
			2		
			2		
			2		
			2		
			2		
			2		
			2		
			2		
			2		
Total for Week					

PAYROLL EXPENSES

Date	Employee	Check #	Acct #	Net Pay	
			16		
			16		
			16		
			16		
Total for Week					

WEEKLY EXPENSE AND INCOME RECORD

Week Ending On _____ , 20 _____

WEEKLY INCOME OR RETURNS

Date	Name and Description	Check # or Cash	Acct #	Amount	
Total for Week					

EXPENSE TOTALS

#	Account	Prior Week Total	Total for Week	Total to Date	
Non-Deductible Expenses					
1	Inventory				
2	Equipment/Property				
3	Loans/Notes Paid				
4	Federal Income Tax				
5	Personal Expense				
6					
	Sub-Total				

#	Account	Prior Week Total	Total for Week	Total to Date	
Deductible Expenses					
7	Advertising				
8	Auto/Truck/Travel				
9	Bank Fees				
10	Contributions				
11	Lodging				
12	Insurance				
13	Interest Paid				
14	Legal/Professional				
15	Meals/Entertainment				
16	Payroll (Net Pay)				
17	Payroll (Deductions)				
18	Postage/Freight				
19	Rent				
20	Repairs/Maintenance				
21	Taxes (Sales)				
22	Taxes (Other)				
23	Supplies/Tools				
24	Telephone/Internet				
25	Utilities				
26					
27					
	Sub-Total				

INCOME TOTALS

#	Account	Prior Week Total	Total for Week	Total to Date
1	Sale of Goods Income			
2	Service/Labor Income			
3	Miscellaneous Income			
4	Returns (deduct)	( )	( )	( )

Prior Week Total	
Total for Week	
Total to Date	

Prior Week Total	
Total for Week	
Total to Date	

EMPLOYEE PAYROLL RECORD

Employee Name:					SS#:				# of Exemptions:		
Address:					Rate of Pay:				Overtime Rate:		

Week ending:	Check #	Hours	OT	Rate	Gross Pay	Federal Tax	Social Secur.	Medicare	State	Total Deduct.	Net Pay
1											
2											
3											
4											
5											
6											
7											
8											
9											
10											
11											
12											
13											
First Quarter Totals											
14											
15											
16											
17											
18											
19											
20											
21											
22											
23											
24											
25											
26											
Second Quarter Totals											
27											
28											
29											
30											
31											
32											
33											
34											
35											
36											
37											
38											
39											
Third Quarter Totals											
40											
41											
42											
43											
44											
45											
46											
47											
48											
49											
50											
51											
52											
Fourth Quarter Totals											
Annual Totals											

EMPLOYEE PAYROLL RECORD

Employee Name: _____ SS#: _____ # of Exemptions: _____

Address: _____ Rate of Pay: _____ Overtime Rate: _____

Week ending:	Check #	Hours	OT	Rate	Gross Pay	Federal Tax	Social Secur.	Medicare	State	Total Deduct.	Net Pay
1											
2											
3											
4											
5											
6											
7											
8											
9											
10											
11											
12											
13											
First Quarter Totals											
14											
15											
16											
17											
18											
19											
20											
21											
22											
23											
24											
25											
26											
Second Quarter Totals											
27											
28											
29											
30											
31											
32											
33											
34											
35											
36											
37											
38											
39											
Third Quarter Totals											
40											
41											
42											
43											
44											
45											
46											
47											
48											
49											
50											
51											
52											
Fourth Quarter Totals											
Annual Totals											

EMPLOYEE PAYROLL RECORD

Employee Name:						SS#:				# of Exemptions:		
Address:						Rate of Pay:				Overtime Rate:		

Week ending:	Check #	Hours	OT	Rate	Gross Pay	Federal Tax	Social Secur.	Medicare	State	Total Deduct.	Net Pay
1											
2											
3											
4											
5											
6											
7											
8											
9											
10											
11											
12											
13											
First Quarter Totals											
14											
15											
16											
17											
18											
19											
20											
21											
22											
23											
24											
25											
26											
Second Quarter Totals											
27											
28											
29											
30											
31											
32											
33											
34											
35											
36											
37											
38											
39											
Third Quarter Totals											
40											
41											
42											
43											
44											
45											
46											
47											
48											
49											
50											
51											
52											
Fourth Quarter Totals											
Annual Totals											

EMPLOYEE PAYROLL RECORD

Employee Name:			SS#:		# of Exemptions:
Address:			Rate of Pay:		Overtime Rate:

Week ending:	Check #	Hours	OT	Rate	Gross Pay	Federal Tax	Social Secur.	Medicare	State	Total Deduct.	Net Pay
1											
2											
3											
4											
5											
6											
7											
8											
9											
10											
11											
12											
13											
First Quarter Totals											
14											
15											
16											
17											
18											
19											
20											
21											
22											
23											
24											
25											
26											
Second Quarter Totals											
27											
28											
29											
30											
31											
32											
33											
34											
35											
36											
37											
38											
39											
Third Quarter Totals											
40											
41											
42											
43											
44											
45											
46											
47											
48											
49											
50											
51											
52											
Fourth Quarter Totals											
Annual Totals											

MONTHLY PAYROLL SUMMARY (Total for All Employees)

Month	Gross Pay	Federal W/H Tax	Social Security	Medicare	State Tax	Net Pay
January						
February						
March						
First Quarter Totals						
April						
May						
June						
Second Quarter Totals						
July						
August						
September						
Third Quarter Totals						
October						
November						
December						
Fourth Quarter Totals						
Annual Totals						

PAYROLL TAX DEPOSITORY RECORD

Month	Federal Tax Withheld	Employee Share of Social Security	Employer Share of Social Security	Employee Share of Medicare	Employer Share of Medicare	Total
January						
February						
March						
First Quarter Totals						
April						
May						
June						
Second Quarter Totals						
July						
August						
September						
Third Quarter Totals						
October						
November						
December						
Fourth Quarter Totals						
Annual Totals						

ANNUAL INVENTORY RECORD

As of December 31, 20 _____

Quantity	Description	Item Number	Unit Price	Total	
				Total	

ANNUAL COST OF GOODS SOLD RECORD

As of December 31, 20 _____

Inventory Value at Beginning of Year	A		
Inventory Added During Year (from Inventory [Acct #1] Annual Total)	B		
Total Inventory Value (A + B) =	C		
Inventory Value at End of Year (from Annual Inventory Record)	D		
Cost of Goods Sold (C - D) =	E		

ANNUAL ACCOUNTS PAYABLE SUMMARY

As of December 31, 20 _____

Vendor's Name	Balance Owed at Beginning of Year		Balance Owed at End of Year	
Total				

ANNUAL ACCOUNTS RECEIVABLE SUMMARY

As of December 31, 20 _____

Customer's Name	Balance Owed at Beginning of Year		Balance Owed at End of Year	
Total				

ANNUAL PROPERTY AND EQUIPMENT SUMMARY

As of December 31, 20 _____

PROPERTY OR EQUIPMENT PURCHASED

Date Purchased	Description	Cost		Depreciation		Balance	
	Totals						

PROPERTY OR EQUIPMENT SOLD

Date Sold	Description	Cost Basis		Selling Expense		Selling Price	
	Totals						

PROPERTY OR EQUIPMENT CASUALTY LOSSES

Date of Loss	Description	Value Before Loss	Value After Loss	Total Loss	
	Totals				

ANNUAL PROFIT AND LOSS STATEMENT

As of December 31, 20 _____

INCOME

Income				
Gross Sales Income = Income Acct #1	A			
Cost of Goods Sold (from Inventory)	B			
Net Sales Income Total (A − B) =	C			
Service Income = Income Account #2	D			
Miscellaneous Income = All Other Income Accounts	E			
Total Income (C + D + E) =	F			

EXPENSES

General Expenses				
Account #	G			
Account #	H			
Account #	I			
Account #	J			
Account #	K			
Account #	L			
Account #	M			
Account #	N			
Account #	O			
Account #	P			
Account #	Q			
Account #	R			
Account #	S			
Account #	T			
Account #	U			
Account #	V			
Account #	W			
Account #	X			
Total Expenses (G+H+I+J+K+L+M+N+O+P+Q+R+S+T+U+V+W+X) =	Y			

Profit or Loss				
Annual Pre-Tax Business Profit or Loss (F − Y) =	Z			

ANNUAL BALANCE SHEET

As of December 31, 20 _____

ASSETS

Current Assets					
	Cash on Hand	A			
	Cash in Bank	B			
	Accounts Receivable	C			
	End of Year Inventory	D			
	Prepaid Taxes/Expenses	E			
	Total Current Assets (A+B+C+D+E) =			F	
Fixed Assets	Equipment (Cost)	G			
	Autos/Trucks (Cost)	H			
	Buildings (Cost)	I			
	Subtotal (G+H+I) =		J		
	Depreciation	K			
	Net Total (J - K) =		L		
	Land (Cost)	M			
	Total Fixed Assets (L+M) =			N	
	Total Miscellaneous Assets			O	
	Total Assets (F+N+O) =				P

LIABILITIES

Current Liabilities					
	Accounts Payable	Q			
	Taxes Payable	R			
	Other Short-term Debts	S			
	Total Current Liabilities			T	
Fixed Liabilities	Long-term Loans Payable	U			
	Other Fixed Liabilities	V			
	Total Fixed Liabilities (U+V) =		W		
	Total Liabilities (T+W) =			X	

Owner's Equity	Net Worth of Business (P – X) =			Y	

ANNUAL SUMMARY FOR TAX PREPARATION

As of December 31, 20 _____

Name of Business:	Accounting Method: ☐ Cash ☐ Accrual
Name of Owner:	Inventory Valuing Method: ☐ Cost ☐ Market Value
Business Address:	Change in inventory method during year? ☐ Y ☐ N
City, State, Zip:	Do you deduct for home office expenses? ☐ Y ☐ N
Social Security # or EIN:	Do you have evidence for deductions? ☐ Y ☐ N
Type of Business:	Is the evidence written? ☐ Y ☐ N
Did you start/acquire business this year? ☐ Y ☐ N	Did you materially participate in business? ☐ Y ☐ N

Income Summary

Acct #	Name of Account	Total
1	Sale of Goods Income	
2	Service/Labor Income	
3	Miscellaneous Income	
	Subtotal Income	
4	Returns (deduct)	( )
	Cost of Goods Sold (deduct)	( )
	Total Net Income	

Accounts Receivable Summary

Value at Beginning of Year	
Value at End of Year	

Accounts Payable Summary

Value at Beginning of Year	
Value at End of Year	

Property and Equipment Summary

Value of Property/Equipment Purchased	
Value of Property/Equipment Sold	

Property or Equipment Casualty Loss Summary

Total Casualty Losses	

Deductible Expenses Summary

Acct #	Name of Account	Total
7	Advertising	
8	Auto/Truck/Travel	
9	Bank Fees	
10	Contributions	
11	Lodging	
12	Insurance	
13	Interest Paid	
14	Legal/Professional	
15	Meals/Entertainment	
16	Payroll (Net Pay)	
17	Payroll (Deductions)	
18	Postage/Freight	
19	Rent	
20	Repairs/Maintenance	
21	Taxes (Sales)	
22	Taxes (Other)	
23	Supplies/Tools	
24	Telephone/Internet	
25	Utilities	
26		
27		
	Total Deductions	

IRS Tax Forms Checklist

Form 1040: *U.S. Individual Income Tax Return*. Must be filed annually by all sole proprietors, partners in a partnership, members of a limited liability company, and shareholders in an S or C-corporation. Do not use IRS Form 1040-A or 1040-EZ.

- **Schedule C**: *Profit or Loss From Business*. Must be filed with IRS Form 1040 by all sole proprietors and a member of a limited liability company electing to be treated as a sole proprietor, unless Schedule C-EZ is filed.
- **Schedule C-EZ**: *Net Profit From Business*. May be filed if gross receipts are under $25,000.00 and expenses are under $2,000.00.

Form 1040-SS: *U.S. Self-Employment Tax Return*. Must be filed annually with IRS Form 1040 by: (1) any sole proprietor who shows $400.00+ income from their business on Schedule C or C-EZ; (2) any partner in a partnership who shows $400.00+ income from their business on Schedule K-1; and (3) any member of a limited liability company who shows $400.00+ income from their business on Schedule K-1, C, or C-EZ.

Form 1040-ES: *Estimated Tax for Individuals (Worksheet)*. Must be used by all sole proprietors, members of limited liability companies, or partners in partnerships who expect to make a profit requiring estimated taxes. Estimated taxes must then be paid and filed quarterly.

Form 1065: *U.S. Return of Partnership Income*. Must be filed annually by all partnerships and limited liability companies that are taxed as partnerships.

- **Schedule K-1**: *Partner's Share of Income, Credits, Deductions, etc*. Must be filed annually by all partners in a partnership and all members in a limited liability company that are taxed as partnerships.

Form 1096: *Annual Summary and Transmittal of U.S. Information Returns*. Must be filed by any business entity that files IRS Form 1099-MISC.

Form 1099-MISC: **Miscellaneous Income**. Must be filed annually by any business entity that has paid any independent contractors over $600.00 annually.

Form 1120: *U.S. Corporation Income Tax Return* or **IRS Form 1120-A**: *U.S. Corporation Short-Form Income Tax Return*. One of these forms must be filed annually by all C-corporations and all limited liability companies that elect to be taxed as a corporation.

Form 1120-S: *U.S. Income Tax Return for an S-Corporation*. Must be filed annually by all S-corporations.

- **Schedule K-1**: *Shareholder's Share of Income, Credits, Deductions, etc*. Must be filed by all S-corporation shareholders.

Form 1120-W: *Estimated Tax for Corporations (Worksheet)*. Must be completed annually by all S- or C-corporations or limited liability companies electing to be taxed as a corporation that expect a profit requiring estimated tax payments.

Form SS-4: *Application for Employer Identification Number*. Must be filed before beginning business by all sole proprietors who will hire one or more employees and all other types of business entities.

Form W-2: *Wage and Tax Statement*. Must be filed annually by all business entities with employees.

Form W-3: *Transmittal of Wage and Tax Statements*. Must be filed annually by any type of business entity with employees.

Form W-4: *Employee's Withholding Allowance Certificate*. Must be provided to employees of any type of business entity. Not filed with the IRS.

Form 940 or 940-EZ: *Employer's Annual Federal Unemployment (FUTA) Tax Return*. Must be filed by all businesses with employees.

Form 941: *Employer's Quarterly Federal Tax Return*. Must be filed quarterly by all businesses with employees.

Form 2553: *Election by a Small Business Corporation*. Must be filed by all S-corporations before starting business.

Form 8109: *Federal Tax Deposit Coupon*. Must be filed monthly by all business entities that have a total payroll tax liability of over $500.00 monthly.

Form 8829: *Expenses for Business Use of Your Home*. Use if necessary and file with annual IRS Form 1040.

Form 8832: *Entity Classification Election*. Must be filed before beginning business by any limited liability company for the purposes of electing to be treated as a corporation, partnership, or sole proprietorship for tax purposes.

Any required state and local income and sales tax forms.

★ Nova Publishing Company ★
Small Business and Consumer Legal Books and Software

Small Business Made Simple Series

Small Business Bookkeeping Systems Simplified
| ISBN 0-935755-74-8 | Book only | $14.95 |

Small Business Payroll Systems Simplified (available late 2003)
| ISBN 0-935755-55-1 | Book only | $14.95 |

Small Business Accounting Simplified (3rd Edition)
| ISBN 0-935755-91-8 | Book only | $22.95 |

Law Made Simple Series

Basic Wills Simplified
| ISBN 0-935755-90-X | Book only | $22.95 |
| ISBN 0-935755-89-6 | Book w/Forms-on-CD | $28.95 |

Divorce Agreements Simplified
| ISBN 0-935755-87-X | Book only | $24.95 |
| ISBN 0-935755-86-1 | Book w/Forms-on-CD | $29.95 |

Living Wills Simplified
| ISBN 0-935755-52-7 | Book only | $22.95 |
| ISBN 0-935755-50-0 | Book w/Forms-on-CD | $28.95 |

Living Trusts Simplified
| ISBN 0-935755-53-5 | Book only | $22.95 |
| ISBN 0-935755-51-9 | Book w/Forms-on-CD | $28.95 |

Personal Legal Forms Simplified (available late 2003)
| ISBN 0-935755-97-7 | Book w/Forms-on-CD | $27.95 |

Small Business Library Series

The Complete Book of Small Business Legal Forms (3rd Edition)
| ISBN 0-935755-84-5 | Book w/Forms-on-CD | $24.95 |

Incorporate Your Business: The National Corporation Kit (3rd Edition)
| ISBN 0-935755-88-8 | Book w/Forms-on-CD | $24.95 |

The Complete Book of Small Business Management Forms
| ISBN 0-935755-56-X | Book w/Forms-on-CD | $24.95 |

Small Business Start-up Series

C-Corporations: Small Business Start-up Kit
| ISBN 0-935755-78-0 | Book w/Forms-on-CD | $24.95 |

S-Corporations: Small Business Start-up Kit
| ISBN 0-935755-77-2 | Book w/Forms-on-CD | $24.95 |

Partnerships: Small Business Start-up Kit
| ISBN 0-935755-75-6 | Book w/Forms-on-CD | $24.95 |

Limited Liability Company: Small Business Start-up Kit
| ISBN 0-935755-76-4 | Book w/Forms-on-CD | $24.95 |

Sole Proprietorship: Small Business Start-up Kit
| ISBN 0-935755-79-9 | Book w/Forms-on-CD | $24.95 |

Legal Self-Help Series

Debt Free: The National Bankruptcy Kit (2nd Edition)
| ISBN 0-935755-62-4 | Book only | $19.95 |

The Complete Book of Personal Legal Forms (3rd Edition)
| ISBN 0-935755-92-6 | Book w/Forms-on-CD | $24.95 |

Divorce Yourself: The National No-Fault Divorce Kit (5th Edition)
| ISBN 0-935755-93-4 | Book only | $24.95 |
| ISBN 0-935755-94-2 | Book w/Forms-on-CD | $34.95 |

Prepare Your Own Will: The National Will Kit (5th Edition)
| ISBN 0-935755-72-1 | Book only | $17.95 |
| ISBN 0-935755-73-X | Book w/Forms-on-CD | $27.95 |

★ Ordering Information ★

Distributed by:
National Book Network
4720 Boston Way
Lanham MD 20706

Shipping/handling: $4.50 for first book or disk and $.75 for each additional
Phone orders with Visa/MC: (800) 462-6420
Fax orders with Visa/MC: (800) 338-4550
Internet: www.novapublishing.com